HC

88 E. Girard Blvd
Kenmore, N.Y.
14217
(716) 876-0007

HOUSES:
Which and When

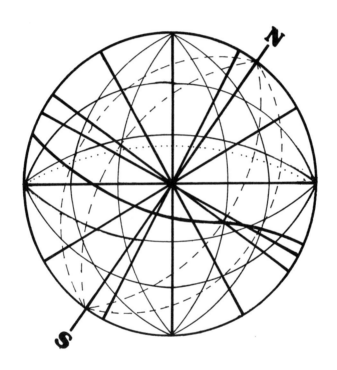

EMMA BELLE DONATH

AFA

Books by Emma Belle Donath:

APPROXIMATE POSITIONS OF ASTEROIDS, 1900-1999
APPROXIMATE POSITIONS OF ASTEROIDS, 1851-2050
ASTEROIDS IN THE BIRTH CHART
ASTEROIDS IN THE BIRTH CHART (revised)
ASTEROIDS IN MIDPOINTS, ASPECTS, AND PLANETARY
    PICTURES
ASTEROIDS IN SYNASTRY
ASTEROIDS IN THE U.S.A. (research)
HAVE WE MET BEFORE?
HOUSES: WHICH AND WHEN
MINOR ASPECTS BETWEEN NATAL PLANETS
PATTERNS OF PROFESSIONS
PLANETARY DECLINATIONS: NORTH AND SOUTH
RELOCATION

First Printing 1989
ISBN Number: 0-86690-377-1
Library of Congress Catalog Card Number: 90-83910

Cover Design:

Published by:
    American Federation of Astrologers, Inc.
    P. O. Box 22040, 6535 South Rural Road
    Tempe, Arizona 85285-0204

"In my Father's house there are many mansions"

TABLE OF CONTENTS

Foreword: *Historical Sketch of the House Systems*
by James H. Holden

FOREWORD:

HISTORICAL SKETCH OF THE HOUSE SYSTEMS

by James H. Holden

The reader may be interested to learn something about the origin of the various systems of house division that will be discussed in this book. They span a period of 2,200 years. During most of that time the majority of astrologers have used whatever system was currently standard without giving much, if any, thought to it. However, there have always been a few astrologers who, for one reason or another, experimented with alternative systems.

Of the systems listed below, only four have achieved "standard" status at one time or another since the birth of horoscopic astrology. These are Sign-House, Alchabitius, Regiomontanus, and Placidus. Sign-House was handed to the world by the inventors of horoscopic astrology. Alchabitius seems to have appealed to the "scientific" instincts of astrologers. Regiomontanus tables were the first to appear in print. And Placidus owes its current leading status to an historical accident. Perhaps the most significant fact that emerges from this is that the original system has survived to the present day.

Sign-House System:
The Sign-House system is the original system of houses devised by the inventors of horoscopic astrology in Alexandria, Egypt, in the third or second century B.C. The astrologer determined the rising sign and it became the first house, the next sign was the second house, the one after that the third house, etc. This system was adopted by the Indians when they imported horoscopic astrology from the West in the second century A.D. It continued in use in the West until the late Middle Ages when it was largely supplanted by the so-called Alchabitius system.

The Sign-House system has three points in its favor: (1) it is the original system, (2) it has been in continuous use since its invention, and (3) it will work in any latitude, unlike the later quadrant systems that develop absurd distortions in higher latitudes and fail utterly in polar regions.

Interestingly, the Sign-House system has been revived anonymously in the Western world in the twentieth century by the makers of guides for the twelve signs of the zodiac.

Equal House System:
Equal House is a further development of the Sign-House system, in which the Ascendant degree becomes the cusp or beginning of the first house and the remaining cusps are at 30-degree intervals from the Ascendant degree. This system was known to Ptolemy and probably to Thrasyllus (first century), but no one mentions an author, so it perhaps goes back to the second century B.C.

Although the Equal House system was more precise, it never supplanted the earlier Sign-House system, but lived side-by-side with it until both of them were abandoned during the Middle Ages in favor of the Alchabitius system.

With the recovery of Firmicus's *Mathesis* in the fifteenth century, Equal House came once more to the attention of astrologers and was adopted by some, most notably Jerome Cardan (1501-1576).

However, it had to contend against the new Regiomontanus system with its printed table of houses.
It lost. In the present century, it has been revived again, this time in England.

Like its elder brother Sign-House, the Equal
House system works equally well at any point on
the globe, thus avoiding the difficulty encoun-
tered by most of its successors in the polar
regions.

Porphyry House System:

The Porphyry House system was the first of
the quadrant systems. It goes back at least to
the astrologer Orion (second century A.D. or
earlier), although it is commonly called the
Porphyry system because it is explained in Chapter 43 of Porphyry's *Introduction to the Tetrabiblos*, written at the end of the third century.

The Porphyry system retains the Ascendant
degree of the Equal House system as the cusp of
the first house, but the astronomical Midheaven
degree is substituted for the original Midheaven
degree, which is the point in dexter square to
the Ascendant degree. The cusps of the intermediate houses are calculated quite simply by trisecting the zodiacal arc of each quadrant.

It never really caught on, although it was
used by a few astrologers in each generation from
the second century A.D. forward. Curiously
enough, its descendant, the Alchabitius system,
did achieve popularity.

Alchabitius House System:

In the fifth century, it occurred to some
Greek astrologer that the trisection of the zodiacal arc from the Midheaven degree to the Ascendant degree could, by analogy, be applied to the
arc of right ascension between those same two
points. At the same time this quadrantal arc was
equal to the semidiurnal arc of the Ascendant degree. It thus appeared that switching from the
zodiacal arc to the corresponding arc of right
ascension would add precision to the trisection.

This procedure appears for the first time in

a horoscope of the year A.D. 428, cited by the astrologer Rhetorius, who flourished around A.D. 505. It passed to the Arabs and was mentioned by several Arab astrologers and astronomers, most notably al-Qabīsī or Alchabitius (d. ca. 967), who mentioned it in his book, *Introduction to the Judgments of the Stars*, which was very popular in its Latin version in the West from the twelfth century on.

Since it required the use of astronomical tables and a little simple calculation, this system appeared to be more "scientific" to its users than the simpler Sign-House or Equal House systems. It steadily gained ground and was probably the leading system by the fifteenth century. However, it rapidly lost its popularity with the advent of the Regiomontanus system. By the end of the sixteenth century, it was virtually forgotten.

Campanus House System:
Campano of Novara, Italy, lived in the latter half of the thirteenth century. He was a learned scholar and mathematician, interested in astronomy, astrology, and medicine, and employed for a number of years as papal chaplain.

The prevailing house system in his day was the so-called Alchabitius system. We do not know whether he was dissatisfied with that system or whether he simply conceived a more elegant one. At any rate, he divided the sky into twelve equal parts that resemble the sections of an orange lying on its side. Campano, who was a skilled mathematician, did not prepare any tables from which the cusps could be taken by inspection, and this undoubtedly prevented his system from gaining wider acceptance, for it was not easy to calculate Campanus cusps prior to the invention of logarithms.

The Campanus system never gained any popularity. It languished as a curiosity until the twentieth century, when Maurice Wemyss, Charles E. O. Carter, and a few other astrologers investigated it. It received its greatest support from Cyril

HOUSES: WHICH AND WHEN

Fagan and his fellow siderealists, although with the decline of interest in siderealism, it has again slipped back into obscurity.

Regiomontanus or Rational House System:

Johann Müller (1436-1476), of Königsberg, Bavaria, was perhaps the foremost mathematician of the fifteenth century. He studied under George von Peurbach (1423-1461) at the University of Vienna, worked for several years at Nürnberg, and was summoned to Rome in 1474 by Pope Sixtus IV to work on calendar reform. Unfortuna-tely, he succumbed to a "pestilential fever" and died in 1476.

Regiomontanus, as he is universally known, was an accomplished astronomer and was also interested in astrology. He studied Ptolemy's *Almagest* and *Tetrabiblos* and thought he recognized in Book 3, Chapter 10, of the latter work an allusion to a system of house division different from the Equal House system. Accordingly, he not only wrote an explanation of this system and his reasons for believing that it was "what Ptolemy had in mind," but he also prepared extensive tables for calculating the house cusps and primary directions. These were the first house tables to appear in print, and from their publication in the 1470's, they rapidly became the accepted standard in Europe.

For two hundred years Regiomontanus reigned supreme. It was the system used by Luca Gaurico, Giuntini, Argol, Morin, Lilly, and Gadbury. But the demise of astrology at the end of the seventeenth century carried Regiomontanus down with it. And, the last prominent seventeenth-century astrologer, John Partridge (1644-1715), had switched to Placidus. When the revival came, things changed.

Morinus House System:

Jean Baptiste Morin (1583-1656) was a medical doctor by education and (from 1630) Royal Professor of Mathematics at the Collège de France in Paris. As an astrologer, he was consulted by many

Emma Belle Donath

prominent people. Morin was a confirmed advocate
of the Regiomontanus system of house division,
but, perceiving that it could not work above the
polar circles, he invented a variant of his own.

The Morinus system is not a quadrant system.
It ignores the Ascendant altogether and uses the
right ascension of the *medium coeli*, or RAMC, as
its fundamental factor. Multiples of thirty
degrees are added to the RAMC, and the resulting
right ascensions are converted to zodiacal longitude by a simple calculation. In general, none
of the cusps so calculated coincide exactly with
those produced by any other system.

Morin described his system as a "universal
rational system." He said it was superior to the
Regiomontanus system because it will work in high
latitudes clear up to the poles. However, despite
his evident enthusiasm for the system, he did not
use it. In fact, its only well-known advocate has
been the modern English astrologer Edward Lyndoe.

Placidus House System:
Placidus de Titis (1603-1668) was professor
of mathematics at Pavia and personal astrologer
to Archduke Leopold William of Austria. Based on
his study of *Tetrabiblos* iii. 10, he believed
that he had recovered the system of house division that he thought Claudius Ptolemy had in
mind. He therefore published, in 1650, an explanation of his system along with the necessary
tables and issued a detailed examination of Placidian directions in thirty nativities of prominent persons.

In one respect Placidus was right. He had
recovered Ptolemy´s method for primary directions. But, his main thesis—that he had also
recovered Ptolemy´s house division system—was
wrong, for Ptolemy had had nothing more in mind
than the Equal House system, which, along with
Sign-House, was standard in his day. At any
rate, Placidus devised a system that was consis-
tent with Ptolemy´s directions for primaries.
However, like all the other quadrant systems, it
fails in polar latitudes.

HOUSES: WHICH AND WHEN

The Placidus system came upon the scene too late to have much of an impact in the seventeenth century. Astrology virtually died out on the Continent by the end of the century. However, it lasted a little longer in England, where the English astrologer John Partridge became a convert to Placidus. During most of the 1700's astrology languished in England, but when it surged up again in the 1780's the Sibly brothers, influenced by Partridge's books, adopted the Placidian system, translated some of Placidus's books, and issued a Placidian table of houses. Other English revival astrologers followed their lead. And, when astrology came back to life in France and Germany around 1900, astrologers in those nations adopted the then current English standard —Placidus.

MERIDIAN HOUSE SYSTEM:

This system is similar to the Morinus system. It was devised by the Australian Zariel (David Cope) in the early 1900's. It is also sometimes called the Axial Rotation system. To find the right ascensions of the house cusps, add multiples of thirty degrees to the RAMC and convert the resulting right ascensions of the cusps to zodiacal longitude with a right ascension table. Like the Morinus system, it is not a quadrant system and will, therefore, work in higher latitudes. In general, the only cusps that coincide with Campanus, Regiomontanus, or Placidus are the Midheaven and the *imum coeli*, or IC.

SOLAR EQUILIBRIUM CHART:

When the birth time is unknown, the astrologer is deprived of the principal tool of horoscopic astrology—the houses. To remedy this lack, he can supply a speculative birth time based upon the native's physical appearance and life circumstances, or he can adopt some arbitrary procedure. The favorite in the twentieth century is the "Solar Chart" or the "Sun-rising Chart." In this chart, the Sun is placed upon the cusp of the first house as if the native had been born at sunrise. The astrologer can then use his favorite house system to derive the cusps of the other houses.

Research has not yet disclosed the inventor of this procedure, but it seems to have originated in the early twentieth century, perhaps among astrologers writing articles on notable persons whose birth times were unavailable. Astrologers of the nineteenth and preceding centuries were more inclined to use speculative birth times. However, the use of a speculative time is risky, as the true time may later become available. It is obviously safer to use an arbitrarily chosen time. The Solar Chart serves that purpose.

The Solar Equilibrium chart is a Solar Chart with Equal Houses. Although it is an outgrowth of the Solar Chart, its principal use is as an adjunct chart to a regular horoscope, since it shows the relation of the other planets to the Sun in a framework of houses.

HAMBURG SCHOOL SYNTHESIS OF 6 HOUSES:

The German astrologer Alfred Witte (1878-1941) invented a new system of astrology, laying heavy emphasis upon hypothetical planets, midpoints, and "planetary pictures." He also made use of a set of six horoscopes utilizing Equal House division: the Earth Horoscope, the Meridian Horoscope, the Moon Horoscope, the Ascendant Horoscope, the Moon's Node Horoscope, and the Sun Horoscope. Thus, he did not propose a new system of house division, but rather a new system of interpretation.

MIDHEAVEN EQUAL HOUSE SYSTEM:

This system, also called "M-House", was proposed by the Astrological Lodge of The Theosophical Society of London in 1952. It is analogous to the Equal House system, but uses the Midheaven degree as the key point. The other cusps are derived by adding multiples of thirty degrees to the Midheaven degree. This is somewhat similar to the Meridian Horoscope of the Hamburg School.

HOUSES: WHICH AND WHEN

OCTOSCOPE:
This is a system of only eight houses (of 45 degrees each) beginning at the Ascendant degree and counted in the clockwise direction. They have the same significations as the first eight of the regular twelve houses. Cyril Fagan (1896-1970) began to write about these in the early 1950's and insisted that they were superior to and older than the usual twelve houses. He preferred to call them "watches" instead of houses. But, despite his original enthusiasm for the Octoscope, Fagan continued to use the twelve-house system for most of his work.

BIRTHPLACE HOUSE SYSTEM:
The German astrologer Walter Koch (1895-1977) published a book in 1960 entitled *Regiomontanus and the Birthplace House System*. It explained the principles of a new house division system. This was followed in 1962 by tables for latitudes 45 to 56 degrees and in 1965 by additional tables for latitudes of 23 to 44 degrees. More extended sets have since been published.

Koch claimed that his system gave more accurate intermediate cusps because they were calculated with the true latitude of the birthplace (whence the name given to the system) instead of with "artificial latitudes" as was the case with the Regiomontanus and Placidus systems. However, this claim, while sincere, was based upon a misconception held by Koch. In fact, his system is no truer to the latitude of the birthplace than Placidus or Regiomontanus. And, like them, it fails in the polar regions.

TOPOCENTRIC HOUSE SYSTEM:
This system was derived experimentally by two Argentine astrologers, A. P. Nelson Page (1919-1970) and Vendel Polich (1892-1980) about 1960. Mathematically, it is a simple variation of the Placidus system, from which its intermediate cusps differ little in lower latitudes. Like the other quadrant systems, it fails in polar latitudes. However, the authors also devised a com-

panion system that is applicable in high latitudes.

FINAL COMMENT:
These are the principal systems of house division that have achieved some measure of success since the invention of astrology. The
youngest is barely thirty years old, while the
oldest goes back two millennia. There is a wide
range of choice.

James H. Holden

September 1989

1

HOROSCOPIC HOUSE SYSTEMS

Of all the astrological problems facing contemporary practitioners, probably the greatest concerns the use of one or more systems of house division. Are house systems to be considered merely mathematical corrections or variations on previous systems, or do they vary according to the philosophy of the originator? Those, and many other questions remain to be answered.

Is any astrology chart without houses like an uncut pizza, too large to handle and too hard to eat? This issue has been debated for the past 2000 years and yet remains unsolved. When an astrologer has decided for houses, he still must determine which one to use.

The premise of this book is that no single house system answers all needs and that each major system was derived to examine a particular set of circumstances, both esoteric and mundane. With these conditions in mind, hundreds of actual examples were observed, data were taken from clients and students alike, and suggestions stated herein were made. This study does not propose to answer all questions about house division and use, merely to add some ideas to the arguments heretofore presented.

Emma Belle Donath

Horoscopes have been called maps, wheels of destiny, planispheres, faces of nature's clock, diagrams of the sky, and other such descriptive titles. Horoscope in Greek is *horoskopos*, or hour mark. Within that framework, houses are variously called places, areas of experience, rooms, foci, sectors, channels, departments of life, geoarcs, watches, arcs, and grounds.

Manly Hall has given a most succinct definition in his book, *The Story of Astrology: "A horoscope is a map or diagram of the heavens cast for a particular moment of time, drawn on paper, and read according to well-established rules."* It is those rules which most astrologers choose to ignore. Only by using the rules established by the originator of each system will we ever be able to understand and evaluate what he had in mind when formulating that particular house division system.

The science of astrology is generally concerned with observing the positions of certain bodies and points in the celestial sphere in relation to earth and with correspondences between those observations and terrestrial events. Since the greater part of the history of astrology has been carried down through various oral traditions its actual origins and overall purpose are truly unknown, but horoscopic astrology or domification is a product of these past 2200 years and some few written records are extant.

For the sake of brevity, only the basic rules of house formulation are included herein, but excellent references for detailed information are included in the Bibliography. Although fixed stars, comets, and other phenomena are quite valid points to observe, this volume will be concerned only with relationships between planets and the twelve major house systems to be discussed.

House divisions are created by mathematically dividing space or time through calculations based on one or another of the great circles of what is called the celestial sphere (Figure 1).

The **celestial sphere** is an enlargement of the

20

sphere of the planet earth to embrace the visible heavens. From any given location on the earth,

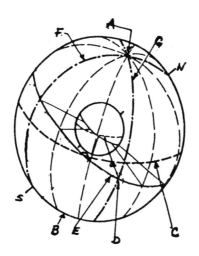

Figure 1.   View of the celestial sphere showing the (A)zenith, (B)nadir, (C)celestial horizon, (D)celestial equator, (E)ecliptic, (F)meridian, and (G)the prime vertical.

the point directly overhead is the zenith and the point directly opposite that is the nadir. At right angles to these points is the horizon, or line which intersects the earth and sky. The visible horizon is a personal view of where sky and land appear meet, while the celestial horizon is a calculated circle representing the horizon as if it were measured from the earth's center and then extended into space.

The celestial equator is a projection of the earth's equator extended out into space. (Right ascension is measured along this great circle.) The ecliptic, or Sun's apparent path around the earth, varies from crossing the celestial equator to moving at an inclination of 23 degrees 26 minutes north or south from it. This inclination is presently decreasing at a rate of fifty seconds

per century and is expected to reach an inclination of 22 degrees 30 minutes by 12,000.

Another major great circle is the **meridian**,
which passes through the zenith, the nadir, and
the north and south poles of the celestial horizon. The **prime vertical** is a great circle which
lies at right angles to the meridian and passes
through the zenith, the nadir, and the east and
west poles or points of the celestial horizon.

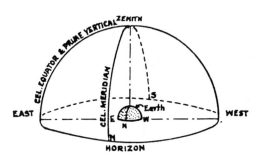

Figure 2. Right hemisphere of the celestial
sphere cut at the celestial horizon.

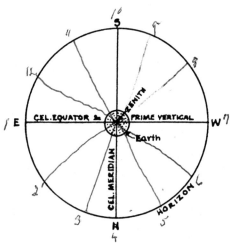

Figure 3. Right hemisphere in the plane of the
celestial horizon, showing a quarter-
ing of the sky.

HOUSES: WHICH AND WHEN

Figures 2 and 3 show cross sections of the celestial horizon, cut to show how these great circles would appear to an observer standing on the planet's surface.

It is only one step from here to drawing a three-dimensional map on a two-dimensional plane such as paper or clay, like the diagram shown in Figure 4.

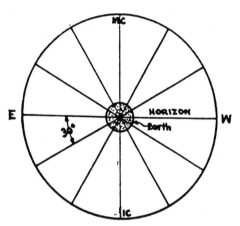

Figure 4. Diagram of the sky cut into twelve equal arcs.

Houses are normally considered as divisions of time, space, and the ecliptic. The primary time-derived houses include Alcibitius, Placidus, Birthplace or KOCH, and Topocentric. Among the houses found by dividing segments of space are Campanus, Regiomontanus or Rational, and Morinus. Houses which rely on divisions of the ecliptic include Sign-House, Equal, Porphyry, Solar Equilibrium, and M-House. Other categories such as quadrant or nonquadrant will be discussed in later chapters.

Key statements for the twelve house systems:

Sign-House - manner of accepting or rejecting
    personal karma, world conditions, and sur-

rounding environment

Equal House - heritage from family members, genetic defects or traits, one-to-one confrontations, and closeness in relationships

Porphyry - clear division between body and soul, way of compartmentalizing spiritual and mundane matters

Campanus - immediacy of mundane conditions and how they affect society, and a timing device

Rational - cosmic views broken down into personal responses, an enhancement of the theory of "as above, so below"

Morinus - path of individual involvement into physical, mental, and spiritual matters

Placidus - goals of life, current psychological understanding, answering of horary and electional questions, and some timing

M-House - manner in which public successes or failures validate self

Solar Equilibrium - each house represents a facet of the incarnating ego or personality

Hamburg - different houses represent everything from personal health to life's purpose

Octoscope - expectation from mundane matters of the day, and a timing device

Birthplace - past, present, and future goals, expected reactions to events and conditions

Planets could be considered as lights which shine through different colored windows (representing the zodiacal signs) into rooms which are carpeted and furnished according to their expected usage (representing horoscopic houses). In one building those rooms may be built according to one set of dimensions while in another equally well-designed building, rooms will be constructed along entirely different lines and furnished in divergent styles. The lights are able to shine as clearly and illuminate as much area in the first situation as in the second, yet what will be seen is quite different. Perhaps that is one way to view horoscopic house systems.

2

SIGN-HOUSE SYSTEM

Ptolemy described a division of the ecliptic which was parallel to the natural zodiac, beginning with the sign on the horizon at birth, and which went around the celestial horizon in twelve increments of thirty degrees each. The Egyptian astrologer and philosopher Petosiris is reckoned as one of the first to have defined and used the rising sign as an important factor in astrology.

Several ancient texts are circulated under the authorship of Petosiris and Nechepso. As was the custom in those days, the actual authors were probably writing under pen names of famous rulers or priests of the past. Nechepso was the name of a king whom Manetho included in the twenty-sixth dynasty listing. The most famous Petosiris was a high priest of Thoth, although many others used that title of "Beloved of Osiris."

The astrological manuscripts which are known fall into four categories: (1)those using astrological omens developed during the Achemenid and Ptolemaic periods in Mesopotamia; (2)others derived from a revelation text in which Nechepso, supposedly guided by Petosiris, sees a vision of horoscopic truths; (3)treatises on astrological botany for medical purposes; and (4)treatises on numerology.

Some of these works quote authors of late antiquity like Hephaestes of Thebes, Proclus, Campestrius, and Lydus. These texts of Petosiris speak of eclipses, heliacal risings of various fixed stars, comets, colors of eclipsed bodies, winds blowing from the four corners of the earth, shooting stars, halos, lightning, rain, and the presence of bodies in various signs of the zodiac. The astrological omens were concerned with length of a native´s life, good and bad times for that person, as well as travel, injury, children, and death circumstances.

In the Sign-House method, the rising sign becomes the first house, and the houses follow in order, being associated with each successive zodiacal sign (see Figure 5). Only whole signs were considered, never sections or increments of same. This was the earliest form of house division found in Egypt and Greece, and is widely used in India even today.

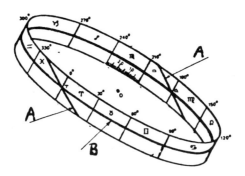

Figure 5.   Diagram of the belt of the zodiac, showing the zodiacal signs of Aries, Taurus, Gemini, Cancer, Leo, Virgo, Libra, Scorpio, Sagittarius, Capricorn, Aquarius, and Pisces in their respective 30-degree arcs of celestial longitude. The celestial equator is marked as (A), the ecliptic as (B).

HOUSES: WHICH AND WHEN

The **Ascendant** is the degree of the zodiac which appears on the eastern horizon at the moment a figure is being cast or at the birth of a person, idea, or association. It is called the rising degree or sign and relates to the first house in a nativity or horoscope. This point can be seen in Figure 5 as the place where line A crosses circle B.

According to Hindu astrologer Shil-Ponde, in his book on *Hindu Astrology,* houses are imaginary space divisions radiating out vertically from any point on the earth's surface, and marking portions of space which are traversed by this point during each 24-hour day as the earth revolves on its axis. The twelve houses overlay the constellations, with the position of each constellation or zodiacal sign remaining constant on the map (see Figure 6).

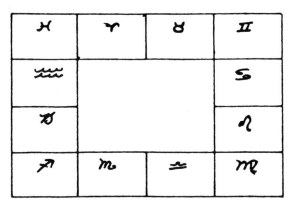

Figure 6.   Typical Southern Indian Rashi or life map or horoscope.

The twelve houses overlay the zodiacal signs, with the first house beginning at the sign where lies the rising degree or Lagna. The cusp of each house is thirty degrees from the preceding house, but the power of each house extends fifteen degrees in each direction from that cusp. In other words, the center of each house is the line of the cusp.

In Northern India, the horoscopic houses run counter-clockwise and in Southern India they run clockwise. Although there are minor differences from one Indian province to another, the basic house meanings do not alter from north to south. The counter-clockwise order is shown in Figure 7, along with cuspal emphasis and major points to be considered.

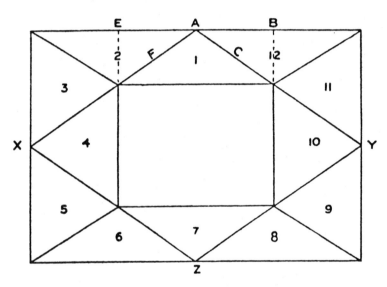

Figure 7. Northern Hindu chart of houses showing bisections of sides of the rectangle, including (A)the Ascendant, (B)cusp of the twelfth house, (C)the beginning of the first house, (E)cusp of the second house, (F)the end of the first house, (X)cusp of the fourth house, (Y)cusp of the tenth house, or Midheaven, and (Z)cusp of the seventh house. Each of the triangles forms a house.

A Western corollary to this type of Sign-House chart is shown in Figure 8. The beginning of the first house is not aligned with the cusp which is drawn on the horizon.

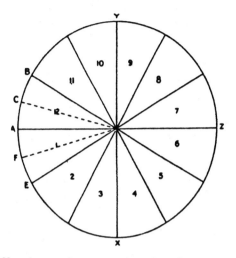

Figure 8. Western house chart, drawn according to Hindu concepts: (A)the eastern horizon, (B)the cusp of the twelfth house, (C)the rising point in Hindu astrology, (E)the cusp of the second house, (F)the end of the first house in Hindu astrology, (X)the cusp of the fourth house, (Y)the cusp of the tenth house, and (Z)the cusp of the seventh house.

Here are some keywords for a Hindu Rashi:

House 1 - activity, appearance, birth, body, build, character, disposition, status, willpower

House 2 - early education, family, imagination, jewels, money, property, quality of speech, source of death, studies

House 3 - appointments, courage, hearing, intelligence, letters, neighbors, royal help, servants, short journeys, younger siblings

House 4 - comforts, conveyances, education, general happiness, house, mother, popularity, real estate

29

House 5 - children, fame, intelligence, karma,
love, prestige, religious practices,
speculation
House 6 - cook, daily foods, debts, disease,
enemies, injury by weapons, loss of
money, misery
House 7 - death, freedom, foreign sojourns, law-
suits, love, public enemies, spouse
House 8 - accidents, chronic diseases, gifts,
legacies, longevity, mental worry,
sex, widowhood for female, wills
House 9 - charities, father, god, grandson,
guru, medicine, travels, worship
House 10- dharma, fame, good deeds, mercy,
philosophical knowledge, occupation
House 11- clothes, elder brothers and sisters,
gains, happiness, jewels, wealth
House 12- assault from the unknown, bed, ex-
penditures, government, loss, repose,
secret enemies

The Hindu Sign-House system relies heavily on
planetary rulerships and the effects caused when
those planets are posited in the various houses.
For example, Saturn placed in one of its natural
houses (tenth or eleventh houses), or in a house
where the zodiacal signs of Capricorn or Aquarius
lay, would be considered very differently than in
Saturn another position. This ancient pattern of
planetary rulerships is still used, with no consideration for the outer planets-Uranus, Neptune,
and Pluto.

Cancer	- Moon/Sun -	Leo
Gemini	- Mercury -	Virgo
Taurus	- Venus -	Libra
Aries	- Mars -	Scorpio
Pisces	- Jupiter -	Sagittarius
Aquarius	- Saturn -	Capricornus

An example of a life chart or Rashi is given
in Figure 9. Sun lies in the first house over
the sign Taurus, so the native will have conveyances and government favor, as well as dominion

over enemies. Venus lives in the second house, giving sexual pleasures and money for clothing and jewels, in addition to an interest in music and drawing.

Jupiter in the third house brings quarrels with sons, but help from neighbors. He will take care of personal health before other matters. Kethu, or South Node, in the fourth house brings worries at home or from the mother.

The status of the father is high, because Saturn lies in its normal house in the sign of Capricorn. Money is spend on religious endeavors and there is an interest in astrology. With the Moon also in the ninth house, this person will be polite and obedient to elderly persons, fond of travel, and religious.

Rahu, or North Node, in the tenth house brings sexual pleasure, wealth, and travel. Mars lies in its sign of Aries in the twelfth house, giving the native some relief from enemies. With Mercury there also, there is some difficulty with the voice and upper chest.

This native was born into a family of note, well-educated, interested in metaphysics, and instrumental in founding a church.

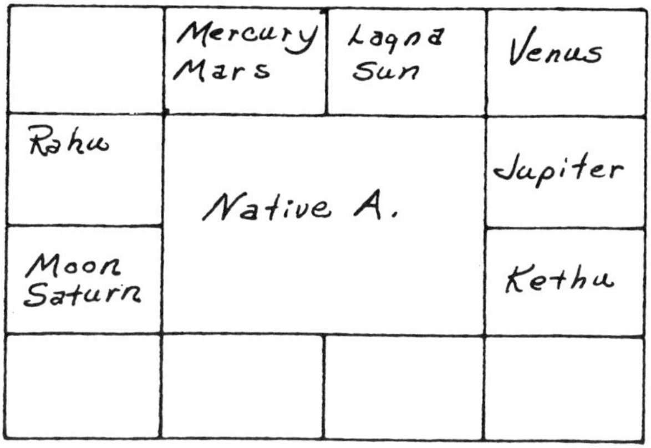

	Mercury Mars	Lagna Sun	Venus
Rahu	Native A.		Jupiter
Moon Saturn			Kethu

Figure 9.   Example horoscope for Native A given in the Hindu Sign-House system, using Lahiri's ayanamsa.

Emma Belle Donath

N. C. Lahiri maintains that Spica at 0 Libra 00 is to be considered as the fiducial point and this system has been adopted by the Indian government as the official astrological stance. So, the horoscope shown in Figure 9 was calculated using Lahiri's ayanamsa.

Of course, no Hindu reading would be complete without including an asterism map and several of the various *vargas*, or divisional maps. The major *vargas* include the *navamsa*, or consideration of marriage and fertility; the *drekana*, for death and longevity; the *dwadasamsha*, describing the bond between past and future lives as well as the parents; the *hora*, for emotional and personal ties, character development, and predictive reactions; the *saptamsha*, to tell one's children's chances of prosperity; the *dasamsha*, for liklihood of realizing ambitions; the *siddhamsha*, for educational opportunities; the *swavedamsha*, for general well-being and prosperity; or the special *trimsamsas* for all females, to tell about childbirth and other female endeavors.

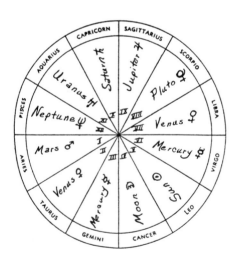

Figure 10.   One contemporary pattern of planetary rulers, with their associated zodiac signs and horoscope houses.

HOUSES: WHICH AND WHEN

Contemporary Western astrologers primarily use the Sign-House system to teach about correlations between zodiacal signs, planetary rulers, and horoscope houses (Figure 10).

There is no set pattern of rules for a modern Western interpretation of the Sign-House system. Therefore, interested proponents must look to the quite comprehensive body of Hindu literature for further direction and information about using this system.

As with the example horoscope (in Figure 9) and the house meanings given herein, traditional use of the Sign-House method does appear to answer the original premise: Delineations given by the Hindu or Sign-House system look for acceptance or rejection of karma and dharma in this incarnation, for conditions into which the native has been born, and for family circumstances which affect the native. The most accurate results obtained from using this system occurred when planetary longitudes were calculated in the fixed zodiac, using Lahiri's sidereal vernal point or positions.

Hellenistic and antique documents which pertain to the Sign-House system normally were concerned with planetary positions calculated in the fixed zodiac or against the true constellations rather than in the tropical zodiac so commonly in use today. It would be difficult to transfer that total body of knowledge into the movable-zodiac system and to judge such a system without decades of empirical testing.

The Sign-House system, particularly when used in the total scope of Hindu or Eastern astrological practices, has a fine track record after over 2000 years of continual use. A quick look at a Rashi or life chart certainly indicates an appreciable amount of valuable information, as shown in this chapter. A total interpretation, complete with at least the most important *vargas,* results in a comprehensive look at the longevity, relationships, ambitions, and religious views of any native. Hindu astrologers, with their unique timing methods, have long been acknowledged to

Emma Belle Donath

have made some of the most accurate predictions which have been pronounced within the worldwide astrological community.

3

EQUAL HOUSE SYSTEM

Described from at least the first century B.C. and noted by Claudius Ptolemy in his *Tetrabiblos*, the equal house-division system remains in use today. The Ascendant degree is taken as the cusp of the first house, with the succeeding house cusps following in thirty-degree arcs along the ecliptic. It varies from Sign-House primarily in that houses may contain more than one zodiacal sign. Neither of these systems breaks down with latitude changes, whether at the equator or in polar regions.

For centuries a square form (Figure 11) continued in favor, with the Ascendant degree placed at the easternmost point of the map. Contemporary Western astrologers seem to prefer circular forms.

Ptolemy's reputation as an authority rests on his thirteen books of the *Almagest* which contain an overview of mathematical astronomy as conceived by his contemporaries. He was born in Egypt, descended from Greek ancestors, held Roman citizenship, and had a world view similar to that of Aristotle.

The recovery and translation of the *Mathesis*, by Firmicus Maternus (ca. A.D. 330-354), was a major factor in recalling equal houses to the attention of European astrologers in the 1400's.

This was the last major astrological writing to come out of that ancient period, probably because of the restrictions imposed by the growing Roman Catholic Church.

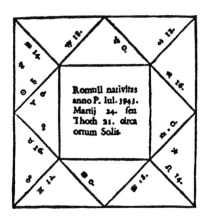

Figure 11. Typical square horoscope form.

Known volumes of the *Mathesis* contain a defense of astrology, astrological elements, the heavens for the present cosmos, meanings for the moon and planets, planets in signs and houses and decans, planets in aspects, career patterns, and a composite of Mesopotamian and Egyptian barbaric spheres. Some historians hold that Firmicus was converted to Christianity around A.D. 346. and ceased his interest in astrology. His keywords for the houses are found in Figure 12.

The English equivalents for these keywords are (from the first house) life, hope, brothers, parents, children, health, spouse, death, God, honors, good angels, and bad angels.

Unlike Sign-House material, there are several sources of data from contemporary astrologers using the equal house method within the Western or tropical system. Two of the best known are Robert Pelletier and Alexandra Mark, both active in New England astrological groups and associations.

HOUSES: WHICH AND WHEN

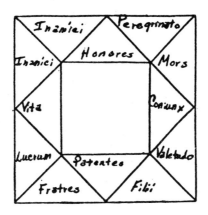

Figure 12. Keywords of Firmicus Maternus.

Mr. Pelletier has been clear about various issues on house division both in lectures and in his book, *Planets in Houses*. He opts for the Ascendant equal house system, considers the cusp of a house as the real power of that house space, applies traditional rulership patterns, considers a planet more in tune with a house when they both operate under the same zodiacal sign, uses the counter-clockwise order of twelve houses, adds the Midheaven as a significant point in a house, and has developed a very workable derivative house pattern.

On the other hand, Mrs. Mark considers the entire thirty-degree arc of each house to be of equal import, gives special emphasis to planets in the fourth and tenth equal houses, advocates mundane (house-to-house) aspects, and accepts the general Western house interpretations.

A third view of Ascendant equal houses comes out of the German-based Hamburg School of Astrology, which has an able spokesman in Roger A. Jacobson. In *Language of Uranian Astrology*, Mr. Jacobson presents an extensive explanation of the Hamburg houses. The Ascendant houses begin with the Ascendant degree on the cusp of the first house and continue around a 360-degree circle with twelve equal divisions of thirty degrees. All planets, asteroids, personal points, transneptunian bodies, midpoints, and planetary pictures within this system define close or personal relationships and the native's immediate environment.

Adaptation of these house meanings used by this author follow. Proximity to the house cusp in question appears to strengthen the activity within that space or house. Rulerships were not used.

House 1 - genetic heritage, status acquired by birth into a particular family, the physical appearance and stance

House 2 - outlook on wealth or poverty gained from parental attitudes, social position of family, inborn talents

House 3 - siblings, cousins near the same age, playmates, close friends, ability to interact with peers

House 4 - nurturing figure (mother, father, or guardian), childhood home, adult bedroom or suite, home altar (rare)

House 5 - romantic liaisons, appearance and demeanor of offspring, recreational needs, hobby mates

House 6 - conduct of co-workers, personal workspace arrangement, preferred working schedule and helpers

House 7 - one-to-one confrontations (pleasant or offensive), legal partners in business or marriage, challengers

House 8 - family resources available for personal use, donors, inheritances, definition of family concerns and response to same

House 9 - friends or relatives among the clergy or educators, relatives living away from the family home, conduct of relatives by marriage

House 10- limiting figure (mother, father, or guardian), authority figures, need for

praise, business connections
House 11- allegiance to causes and organizations, adult friendships, fellow club or lodge members, acquaintances
House 12- ties within the medical fraternity, hidden enemies, secret unions or ties, special confidant, priest confessor

Tropical
Equal House

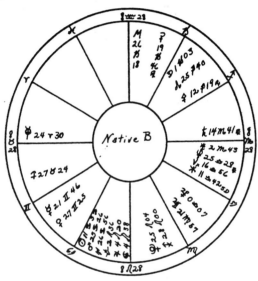

Figure 13. Example horoscope of Native B in the equal house system.

The native shown in Figure 13 is a young man born into a prestigious Southern family (Kronos in the first house and Pluto-Zeus in the fourth), only son (Vesta-Hades-Jupiter near the fourth house cusp) of an adoring mother and grandmother (Leo on the fourth house cusp with Ceres in the ninth of worship), heir of one uncle's not inconsiderable fortune (Pallas-North Node in the eighth), manager of an exclusive men's shop in his early twenties (Neptune-Poseidon in the

Emma Belle Donath

sixth), late earner of a degree in business man-
agement and worldwide traveler (Ceres-Midheaven
in the ninth), handsome bachelor (Cupido-Apollon
in the fifth house), oft engaged without yet
being wed (Juno near the seventh cusp and Saturn
in the seventh house), and beloved nephew of
several successful pairs of uncles and aunts
(Sun-Mars-Uranus-Jupiter in the third house).

An excellent conversationalist, he is able to
talk superficially about any number of subjects,
but devises ways to avoid long-term commitments
or restrictions (Jupiter square Juno). He can
fly off the handle when provoked, but is careful
never to antagonize those who pay the bills (Mars
conjunct Uranus countered by Mercury conjunct
Venus in the second house) for creature comforts
and luxuries.

He commands a certain respect within the
workplace, always having attractive surroundings
plus a position of authority (Neptune trine
Venus). Co-workers need to be "blind" to his
faults or errors (Mars-Uranus square Neptune).
If these conditions are not met, he moves on to
greener fields. The same is true in romantic
liaisons.

This brief delineation shows one way of
looking at equal house charts as a view of the
original premise of family heritage, one-to-one
confrontations, and general relationships. A
more intensive analysis may be made of this individual from birth data given in the Appendix.

4

PORPHYRY HOUSE SYSTEM

Porphyry defended the first unequal system of house division in his *Introduction to the Tetrabiblos*, but it was probably invented by a little-known astrologer named Orion who lived in the prior century (ca. second century A.D.). This system is commonly attributed to Porphyry because his advocation brought it to the attention of his peers.

In this system, the Ascendant degree is placed on the first house cusp and the *Medium Coeli* is located on the cusp of the tenth house. The Midheaven (*Medium Coeli*) often falls into the ninth or tenth house with equal houses because the tenth house cusp is set at ninety degrees from the Ascendant (dexter square to Ascendant).

Intermediate Porphyry houses are calculated by trisecting the quadrant between the Midheaven and Ascendant and then the quadrant between the Ascendant and the *Imum Coeli*, or point directly below the Midheaven. Houses opposite to these calculated tenth, eleventh, twelfth, first, second, third, and fourth houses are equal in degrees of arc to their opposite houses (see Figure 14). The great house circles meet at the poles of the ecliptic. This system is not affected by precession but it does break down at the north and south poles. It is not projected onto the ecliptic, but is calculated from the ecliptical longitudes.

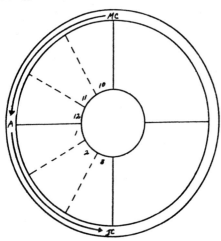

Figure 14. Quadrants divided in the Porphyry house system.

The *Medium Coeli* is calculated as the point overhead where the meridian crosses the ecliptic. Astronomers call the point which is ninety degrees from the Ascendant the *culmination.*

Porphyry also argued that Ptolemy wrote of beginning the emphasis of each house five degrees before the cusp and extending for twenty-five degrees into that house. This theory was used by Porphyry and by numerous other astrologers for centuries. There is debate about this issue today.

Who was this man called Porphyry? Perhaps a look at his background and philosophy will give clues to explain his thoughts and writings. He was born to a native of the Phoenician city of Tyre called Malchus and named after his father. But, Malchus-son-of-Malchus (A.D. 232-306) became entranced by Hellenistic teachings and eventually changed his Semitic name to Greek *Basileus* (king) and later to *Porphyrius* (the purple clad), combining these Hellenistic inclinations with his

HOUSES: WHICH AND WHEN

Phoenician heritage.

Porphyry was a pupil of Neoplatonist scholar Plotinus (A.D. 205-270), who had himself studied under Ammonius Saccas of Alexandria, who also counted Origen among his pupils. The former was later to be known as an antagonist of the growing Christian church, while Origen became the foremost spokesman for the catechetical Christian school in Alexandria. Both were students of the esoteric traditions. In turn, Porphyry was the teacher of Iamblichus, and thus ended the great Neoplatonist tradition.

Neoplatonism concerns itself with methods of divine revelation and unfolding in the world of man. From the fullness of knowledge emerged a creator and all else is dross or overflow. Their creation stories are gnostic in origin, being primarily concerned with the fall of soul or spirit into matter and its ability to return to the upper spheres. Porphyry was quoted as saying that the human soul is a receptacle for either gods or demons (*Ad Marcell, XXI*).

Critics accused Porphyry of practicing magic, even of inducing trance states for he was a natural mystic and had studied Eastern *raj-yoga* for a number of years. One of his greatest disappointments was in not reaching a state of ecstasy before the age of sixty. Porphyry devoted his life to considerations of the bearing of philosophy on practical life. He held that the soul should, as far as possible, be freed from bonds of matter, and recommended abstinence whenever possible.

As with many Neoplatonists, Porphyry praised Christ while disparaging the religion established as Christianity. Noted theologian Apollinaris of Laodicea (A.D. 310-390) wrote thirty volumes against Porphyry. Apollinaris held a trichotomist view of man, supported the doctrine of Nicaea, was anti-Arianist, accepted full union of humanity and divinity in Christ, and saw Jesus as God enfleshed rather than incarnated.

Porphyry was a consummate organizer. He

grouped the sayings of Plotinus into six dis-
courses of nine tractates each in the *Enneads of
Plotinus*, he systematized astrological houses to
represent light and darkness, he established an
order of life which had the aim of purification,
he constituted man as a triad of being and life
and intelligence, he ordered Mithric teachings
into allegories, he structured the world into the
five universals of genus and species and differ-
ence and property and accident, and he authored
an introduction to Aristotle's *Categories.*

Is it any wonder then, that Porphyry saw fit
to give import to a point lying above the horizon
and treat it as representative of the soul of man
cast down into matter? He was concerned with
transcending the mundane and one way of doing
this was to show an enormous visual gap between
the two vertical angles of a horoscope, marking
the distance between a higher heaven (Midheaven)
and earth (*Imum Coeli*) or man's place of physical
birth.

In view of Porphyry's interest in spiritual
matters, it seems logical to use the house system named for him in esoteric delineations. One
view of esoteric or metaphysical astrology considers individuals as being probationers or
average men, seekers on the path of inner knowledge or humans, and initiates of a particular
discipline or disciples. There are schemes of
planetary rulerships for these three types of
natives. One scheme is shown in Table I, although there are others more widely used. The
works of Alice Bailey and Dr. Douglas Baker
contain discussions about esoteric astrology.

Planets are divided into sacred and non-
sacred categories. Vulcan, Mercury, Venus,
Jupiter, Saturn, Uranus, Neptune, and possibly
Transpluto are considered to be sacred, or bodies
clothing initiated logoi. The Sun, Moon, Earth,
Mars, and the Asteroids, including Pluto, are
classified as non-sacred planets inhabited by
logoi who have not passed five cosmic initiations
or tests.

TABLE I. ESOTERIC PLANETARY RULERSHIPS

House	Cusp-Sign	Man	Human	Disciple
1	Aries	Mars	Mercury	Sun
2	Taurus	Vulcan	Saturn	Venus
3	Gemini	Mercury	T/pluto	Vulcan
4	Cancer	Moon	Neptune	Ceres+
5	Leo	Sun	Jupiter	T/pluto
6	Virgo	Ceres+	Moon	Neptune
7	Libra	Venus	Uranus	Saturn
8	Scorpio	T/pluto	Mars	Mercury
9	Sagittarius	Jupiter	Vulcan	Uranus
10	Capricornus	Saturn	Sun	Mars
11	Aquarius	Uranus	Venus	Jupiter
12	Pisces	Neptune	Ceres+	Moon

+Ceres represents the asteroid belt here.

In esoteric astrology, an individual first learns to control his reactions to the planets as they rule his affairs from the each house, and houses are considered to be material prisons. Man is seen as a soul inhabiting a personality which is made up of physical, etheric, emotional, and mental planes. Sacred planets aid in fusing soul and personality aims while non-sacred planets are not able to help in this way.

Keywords for houses considered by humans and disciples include the following:

House 1 - causal body incarnated, creation of a usable personality
House 2 - ability to utilize prana, aspiration and illumination
House 3 - humility, response to soul expression, wisdom used daily
House 4 - custodian of a living essence, harmony of form, working out natural law
House 5 - occultism, awareness of true identity, selflessness
House 6 - synthesis of feminine traits, cosmic womb, revelation, purification

House 7 - legislation, binding of the various
bodies, unions, choices
House 8 - major separations, death, karma and
economy, subdued desire nature
House 9 - search for the unknowable, focus of
discipleship
House 10- unfoldment of divine plan, initiation,
synthesis, becoming one of the elect
House 11- freedom from personality control, to
know the soul´s purpose
House 12- dissolution, detachment, death of the
personality

The gentleman whose horoscope is shown in
Figure 15 was reared in a home where theosophical traditions were taught and has long expressed
a deep interest in metaphysical studies. Upon
visiting this country a few years ago, he recon-
structed his horoscope according to the birthplace system of houses and suddenly found that he
was reacting outside the framework of his normal
patterns, even when factors pertaining to relocation had been calculated. His only purpose in
traveling was to study under a master of Oriental
healing currently living in New York City.

Tropical
Porphyry

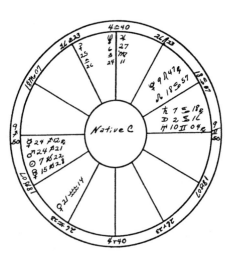

Figure 15.   Native C shown in Porphyry system.

HOUSES: WHICH AND WHEN

Shortly after altering his birth map, this native found himself immersed in a dearth of information and concern about investments and resouces. He was even waking during the night worrying about money, something which had never occurred before. Since this had not been the reason for financing a lengthy stay abroad, he returned home, where the problem continued. After hearing about changes which can occur by accepting a house system, he altered his birth map to Porphyry houses in order to better accomplish his life´s purpose.

Under the Porphyry system, his natal Sun lies in the first house, denoting an event-filled life where honor and mutual respect are paramount in relationships. He is clear-sighted and enterprizing, healthy, and able to express fully. When Sun was moved into the second house, he became cautious and uncertain about goals.

Venus also lies in the space of discipleship, signifying that arts bring spiritual harmony. Another planet in its most spiritual position is Saturn, showing that harmony and balance are not mere words to this man but are qualities exemplified by various archetypes which he attempts to emulate. He sees relationships as karmic fulfillments.

Uranus in the seventh house brings opportunities to be diplomatic and tactful. He currently dates a woman of a totally different faith and cultural background. Mercury on the human or seeker level shows a desire to share opinions or concepts with fellow students. Mental alertness is obvious, but his innate intuitive abilities are well-screened.

Only Mars, Jupiter, and Pluto are in their houses of mundane rulership. Thus, aggressiveness must be changed into assertiveness, cheerfulness into strength of character, and tension into transcendence as this man continues toward discipleship on the spiritual path.

According to esoteric lore, the rising sign shows goals and purposes for the immediate incarnation. His rising sign is in tropical Sagittarius, with mundane ruler in the ninth house, seeker ruler in the first house, and disciple ruler in the seventh house. How is this person to be judged? That is always a most difficult decision. However, with a number of planets in their discipleship positions, it would be understandable to consider this man as being on the path of aspiration. The Midheaven indicates the soul, which in this case is bordered by Neptune and Jupiter, both sacred planets of enlightenment and illumination. Its spiritual ruler is Uranus, posited in the seventh house.

He appears to be growing and developing through the process of continuing study and exloration of various relationships. Birthdata are available for Native C in the Appendix, so that other systems may be erected and analyzed.

5

CAMPANUS HOUSE SYSTEM

Canon Johannes Campano da Novare (A.D. 1233-1296) was a noted astronomer, mathematician, papal chaplain, and physician for Urban IV (A.D. 1261-1264) to Boniface VIII (A.D. 1294-1303). In addition to authoring volumes on astronomy and mathematics, Campano invented a system of house division which yet carries his name.

The prevailing system for thirteenth-century astrologers was one attributed to the Arabic scholar al-Qabisi (ca. A.D. 950) who was a recognized authority on Ptolemy's *Almagest* and author in his own right. The system which carries a Latinized version of his name involves trisecting the Midheaven to Ascendant arc in right ascension (then the Ascendant to IC arc) and projecting these house circles onto the ecliptic. European revival of the Alcibitius system is attributed to English scholars like Roger of Hereford (ca. A.D. 1176) who translated Arabic documents for Western use.

For whatever reason, Campano devised another house system. He divided the prime vertical into twelve equal sections of space. These house circles were projected onto the ecliptic, forming twelve houses unequal in zodiacal longitude (see Figure 16). Campano retained the Ascendant on the first house cusp and Midheaven on the tenth,

but the aim was to put planets into their appro-
priate space with little concern for zodiacal
positions, which implies that houses are superior
to longitude in evaluating planetary strengths.
Signs and aspects became secondary to house positions. The system breaks down at the poles.

Tables for Campanus houses were not published
until A.D. 1495, and they were little used until
adopted by astrologers of the Western sidereal
school in the twentieth century. Notable ex-
ceptions were Fine (A.D. 1494-1555) and Bates of
Malines (ca. A.D. 1292). Bates translated a
number of Arabic astronomical treatises and even
wrote a commentary on one of them. In his own
treatise on the astrolabe, Bates discussed the
question of deriving lines for celestial houses.

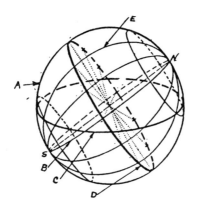

Figure 16. Celestial sphere great circles used to
calculate Campanus houses are the (A)
meridian, (B)horizon, (C)ecliptic, (D)
prime vertical, and (E)a house circle.

Cyril Fagan, Commander R. Firebrace, Maurice
Wemyss, Donald Bradley, and Carl Stahl were among
the contemporary pioneers imploring a return to
constellational considerations in astrological
practice. They advocated use of the Campanus
twelve-house, counterclockwise system with *in
mundo* (house) aspects both for natal analysis and
for mundane timing. Others who later accepted

parts of this concept include Charles Jayne, Edward Johndro, and Dane Rudhyar.

Wheels are drawn into foregrounds, middle-grounds, and backgrounds as shown in Figure 17. Grounds extend from half the arc of a preceding house into half of the degrees of a following house. So, each house cusp falls in the center of its respective ground (ie, foreground 1 falls in the last half of the twelfth house and the beginning half of the first house).

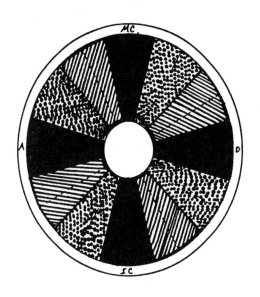

Figure 17. Diagram with foregrounds solid, middlegrounds striped, and back-grounds dotted.

Specific rules hold for reading the grounds. Great import is given to planets falling in any foreground. These planets are *in mundo* conjunction, square, or opposition to each other regardless of longitude. The farther a planet lies from an angle, the weaker is its influence, especially in middlegrounds 2 and 5.

General meanings for a sidereal natal map set in Campanus houses, with Fagan's *ayanamsa*, are:

House 1 - animation, disposition, health, poten-
tial for good fortune, vitality
House 2 - agonies of death, imprisonment, revolt,
thoughts, violence, wars, wealth, work
House 3 - healing abilities, intellect, instruc-
tors, letters, patronage, prophetic
dreams, relatives, religious rites
House 4 - curious secrets, home or house, old
age, parents, real estate, thrift
House 5 - banquets, childbirth, concubines,
offspring, pleasures, speculation
House 6 - completing matters, grief, hospitals,
illness, persecution, servants, worry
House 7 - companionship, duels, encounters,
fines, law, spouse, strife, union
House 8 - dowry, inheritance, legacies, rest,
meditation, unpretentious people
House 9 - courts, education, philosophy, publications, science, voyages, wit
House 10- accounting, credit, father, gain,
honor, merchants, morality, power
House 11- ambassadors, favorites, friends, hopes,
wishes fulfilled
House 12- base of problems, dawning, persecution,
private struggles, secret enemies,
sleep, worries

Other charts normally erected in Campanus
houses are *solars, lunars, demi-* and *quarti-
solars* and *lunars, anlunars,* and four ingresses.
Returns are set for the moment the Sun (or Moon)
returns to the exact position which it occupied
at the onset of a person, place, or thing. Returns calculated without factoring precession are
revolutions and are different from returns.

Ingress charts are set for the moment the Sun
enters sidereal Aries, Cancer, Libra, and Capricorn each year and are called *Arisolars, Can-
solars, Libsolars,* and *Capsolars.* They are
usually erected for major capitals of the world
to determine political, economic, and cultural
trends for the ensuing year.

As these data are moved about the world and
progressed via a progressed sidereal solar return

method (PSSR), current events are indicated by foreground planetary emphases. Figure 18 shows general trends for the United States as represented by its capital and officials.

Sidereal (Fagan)
Campanus

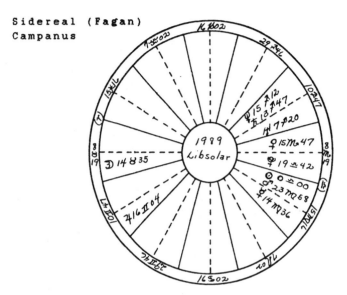

Figure 18. Libsolar for October 18, 1989, at 00:14:30 GMT Washington (38N53/77W50).

According to this Libsolar, American public opinion underwent drastic shifts (Moon in the first house and foreground 1). Feelings fluctuated wildly, vascillating from joy to despair as news arrived of disasters and triumphs.

European allies and open enemies both went out of the way to exert charm and optimism for future contact while crime marched happily on, with drug sales growing daily (Venus in the seventh and Pluto in the sixth houses, both in foreground 7). For the first time in history, an official moratorium was called on naval action because of the extraordinary number of accidents occurring on American naval vessels (see Pluto in the sixth house of armed forces and in foreground 1 as well).

Emma Belle Donath

Sidereal
Campanus

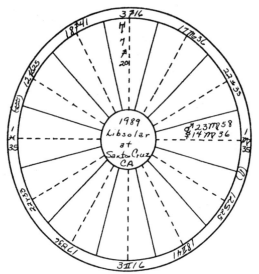

Figure 19. Libsolar of 1989 set for Santa Cruz,
CA (36N58/122W01), epicenter of a
major earthquake that day.

Sidereal   Sidereal
Campanus   Campanus

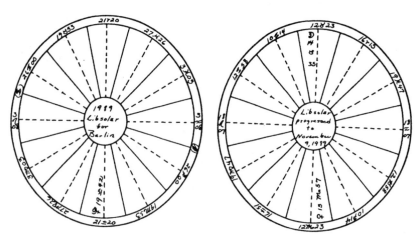

Figure 20. Libsolar of 1989 set for Berlin
(52N30/13E23), PSSR to November 9, 1989.

HOUSES: WHICH AND WHEN

An earthquake of magnitude 6.9 Richter Scale struck the greater San Francisco area just as rush-hour traffic was crossing bridges and major interstates, sections of which collapsed. Few were killed in relation to the property damage sustained in a heavily populated area (Figure 19). No one in the stands was killed or seriously injured at a World Series game in Candlestick Park. This natural catastrophe caught public attention, but caused little loss of life.

Sidereal
Campanus

Sidereal
Campanus

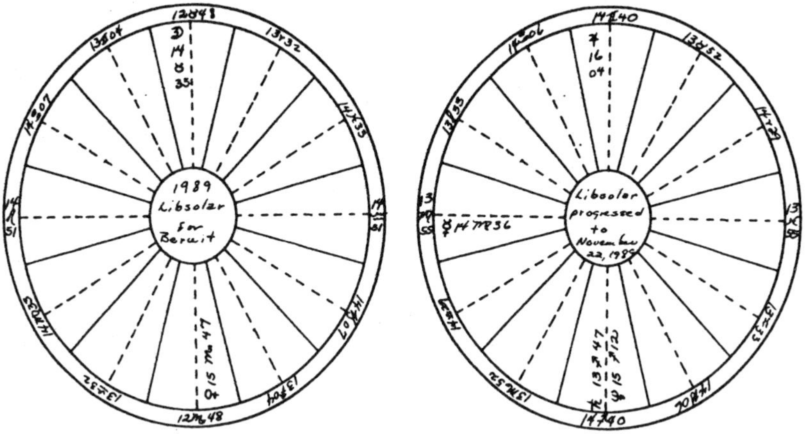

Figure 21. Libsolar of 1989 set for Beruit (33N53/35E30), PSSR to November 22, 1989.

The Libsolar in Berlin shows major upheaval in real estate or government land (Pluto in the fourth house and foreground 4 in Figure 20). The Berlin Wall, symbol of a divided Germany for 28 years, came down. As the Libsolar progressed to November 9, Moon and Venus moved into foregrounds 10 and 4, showing fluctuation in official policy and rejoicing by the free world.

The Moon-Venus *in mundo* opposition is shown in the Libsolar in Beirut, Lebanon, where people

55

first rejoiced at the election of a new president and later mourned his assassination (Figure 21, with foreground 10 Jupiter opposing foreground 4 Saturn and Neptune).

The Libsolar set for Malta indicated major upheaval in talk of properties or boundary lines (Pluto in the third house and foreground 4 in Figure 22). However, the PSSR Libsolar for December 3 shows Uranus in the fourth house and in foreground 4, indicating sharp differences and responses of public opinion to what the attending American and Russian presidents decided at this summit conference.

Sidereal
Campanus

Sidereal
Campanus

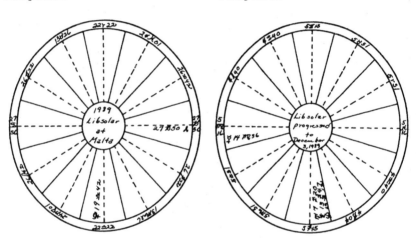

Figure 22. Libsolar of 1989 set for the Island of Malta (35N52/14E25), PSSR to December 3, 1989.

6

RATIONAL HOUSE SYSTEM

Johannes Molitoris de Kunigsberg (A.D. 1436-
1476), or Johann Müller, was better known by the
pseudonym of Regiomontanus. His extensive early
training led to receiving a bachelor's degree at
age 15 and a master's at 21. In 1457 he became a
member of the faculty of the University of Vienna
and a colleague of astronomer George Peurbach.

These two men translated numerous documents,
including Ptolemy's *Syntasis*. Their *Epitome* was
published after Peurbach's death. Both men became aware of the need for additional rules gov-
erning measurement of geometrical figures and
determined to prepare at least one treatise on
geometry. Much of this, plus a work on triangles,
was finally published under the authorship of
Regiomontanus, some even posthumously.

Meanwhile, Regiomontanus was becoming a mathematician of acclaim as he lectured on Muslim
mathematics at the University of Padua in 1464,
published a table of longitudes of celestial
bodies in 1467, traveled to Hungary to collect
Greek manuscripts in 1468, began a lengthy comment on the effect of comets in 1472, and printed
a number of calendars.

In 1471 he had the foresight to request
residency from the city council of Nuremberg.
After this plea was granted, Regiomontanus es-

tablished his own printing press in order to pub-
lish German and Latin textbooks.   Out   of this
effort came an ephemeris for the years A.D. 1475
to 1506. Christopher Columbus   took a copy of
this book on his fourth voyage to the new world
and used the information   therein to predict the
lunar eclipse of February 29, 1504. Knowledge of
this phenomenon frightened hostile Indian tribes
in Jamaica into submission.

     Regiomontanus became known to the titular
Patriarch of Constantinople while he was yet
Cardinal Bessarion.   In 1475 the mathematician
par excellence was called to Rome to assist in
revising the   incorrect ecclesiastical calendar.
Unfortunately, he died from some unknown fever
before completing this task.

     In his study of Ptolemy's astrological works,
Regiomontanus thought there was mention of a system of house division different from the equal
houses.   His   resultant house tables were the
first to appear in print and thus were rapidly
accepted throughout the European astrological
community.   He cut the celestial equator into
thirty-degree intervals from the First Point of
Aries and then projected these points onto the
ecliptic via great house circles. Regiomontanus
explained that he used the celestial equator
rather than the prime vertical because it represented the daily motion of the earth depicted in
the heavens.

     This system, called Rational Houses, repre-
sents a trisection of space dealing with daily
motion or time as an important factor. He saw
houses as mundane aspects of a celestial sphere.
The system is affected by precession, has twelve
divisions, moves counterclockwise, and breaks
down at the polar regions.

     Pre-Reformation greats who adhered to the
system of Regiomontanus included Morin, Gadbury,
Lilly, Bacon, and Cardan.   Culpeper used it for
twelve-house decumbitures or horaries but he used
equal houses with his eight and sixteen division
charts.   Much of the astrological work of that
period concerned illnesses and judgments for

diseases and death. A typical rational figure erected for the onset of a disease, or the time when the patient took to his bed, was called a decumbiture. An example of this type of horary is given in Figure 23.

Tropical
Regiomontanus

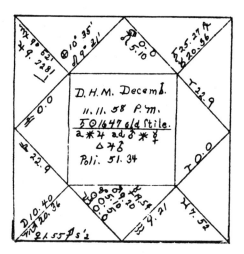

Figure 23. Example decumbiture (horary of a disease onset) of Culpeper.

According to Culpeper, disease was foretold through planets, aspects, or rulerships concerning houses six, seven, and twelve. His process is quite lengthy, but one admonition given to students concerned gathering of medicinal herbs at auspicious times. Culpeper preferred to have planets in the signs which they ruled for the best treatment of the herbs, but if the planets could not be in their homes, Culpeper suggested they should occupy houses in which they found joy or were delighted, as shown in Table II. Lilly also talked much of the mundane houses in which planets were joyful or rejoiced. It is a concept which is practically ignored today.

TABLE II.

Planet	Culpeper Houses of Joy
Sun	Fourth, Ninth, Eleventh
Moon	Third, Seventh
Saturn	First, Eighth, Twelfth
Jupiter	Second, Ninth, Eleventh
Mars	Third, Sixth, Tenth
Venus	Fifth, Twelfth
Mercury	First, Sixth

Schwickert is one of the few contemporary astrologers who uses the Rational House System of Regiomontanus in his counseling or in research. With the advent of computer programs giving a variety of house divisions, perhaps more people will take this opportunity to study some of the classical systems.

Some of the clearest definitions of house meanings have been given by Lilly who considered horoscopic houses to represent the quality of events and of life in general. He looked at houses as extending from the cusp of one to the cusp of the next, not flowing over the cusps or house lunes. As with planets and signs, each house was assigned a color, cosignificators, and places of joy for certain planets. These colors, joys, and significators are given in Table III.

Nativities were delineated under different rules than those used for horaries, disease, electionals, or mundane horoscopes cast to determine the state of the nation or of the world. Both signs and houses were considered to rule or contain parts of the human body and some of the rulerships seem to overlap, while others are quite different from those which are considered today. The lists given here were typical for the times in which Lilly lived.

HOUSES: WHICH AND WHEN

TABLE III.

House	Color	Significator	Joy For
1	white	Aries,Saturn	Mercury
2	green	Taurus,Jupiter	Moon
3	sorrel	Gemini,Mars	-----
4	red	Cancer,Sun	-----
5	gold	Leo,Venus	Venus
6	black	Virgo,Mercury	Mars
7	coal	Libra,Moon	-----
8	green/ black	Scorpio,Saturn	-----
9	green/ white	Jupiter,Mars	Sun
10	red/ white	Capricorn,Mars	-----
11	saffron	Aquarius,Sun	Jupiter
12	green	Pisces,Venus	Saturn

Sample keywords for houses in the Rational House System are as follows:

House 1 - head and face of person, general state of life, countenance

House 2 - neck of person, estate or fortune, movable wealth, monies owed or on loan, second in a duel

House 3 - shoulders and arms and hands, kin, siblings, rumors, letters, travel

House 4 - breasts and lungs, fathers, land, castles, old age, towns, end of a matter or thing

House 5 - stomach and liver and heart, child, ambassadors, pregnancy, taverns, banquets, love

House 6 - belly and intestines, servants, slaves, cattle, sickness, tenants, uncles, health

House 7 - haunches and navel, marriage, spouse, public enemies, lawsuit defendant,

quarrels, peace or war
House 8 - hemorrhoids and gall bladder, dowry,
          death, estates, adversary in duel,
          fears, heir(s)
House 9 - hips and thighs, voyages, clergy,
          dreams, educations, relatives by
          marriage
House 10- knees and thighs, commanders, mother,
          honor, dignity, empire or country
House 11- legs, trust, confidence, praise,
          friends, counselors
House 12- feet, private enemies, large animals,
          sorrow, imprisonments, suffering

An example horoscope set in the Regiomontanus
or Rational System is shown in Figure 24. This
is the nativity of a woman who became a broad-
casting executive before age 30, single parent,
divorced, well-rated documentary producer, and
child of a diabetic and an alcoholic. She was
born into a show business family, with no lack of
monies, eclectic tastes, and erratic tempers.

Tropical
Regiomontanus

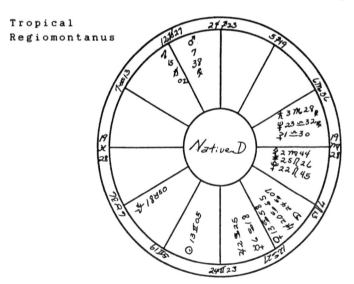

Figure 24. Natal horoscope for Native D.

7

MORINUS HOUSE SYSTEM

Jean Baptiste Morin de Villefranche (A.D. 1583-1656) became a doctor of medicine, professor of mathematics at Collège de France, and learned astrologer. His astrological expertise was attributed to having studied with a Scotsman named Davison. Morin authored many books, including the famous *Astrologica Gallica* and *Astrologicarum donorun cabala detecta a Jean Baptista Morino.* In the cabbala on astrological houses, Morin explains his reason for preferring the logic of Regiomontanus over the deductions of other astrologers who derived the equal house, Porphyry, Alcibitius, and Campanus divisions in use by his contemporaries.

Morin was impressed by the Rational System because its divisions clearly defined positions above and below the horizon. He felt strongly that the beginning of a house (cusp or lune) was its strongest point and must be defined as such. This was especially true of the Midheaven, which does not always lie on a house cusp in equal houses. The breakdown of existing house systems in polar regions bothered Morin, so he revised the Regiomontanus calculations into what has been called a Rational and Universal System of Domification (Morinus system). In this new system, Morin added multiples of thirty degrees to the

right ascension of the *Medium Coeli* and then converted the results into zodiacal longitude. Latitude does not affect the resultant house cusps
at all and the Ascendant is largely ignored.

His major argument was that other astrologers
were attempting to divide the sky in relation to
the earth rather than dividing the earth with respect to the heavens. Thus, he argued that a division based on the equator, and thence on the
celestial equator, was more logical and more in
keeping with the demands of nature (Figure 25).
The four cardinal points (north, south, east, and
west) are considered symbolic of the four angles
of a horoscope (fourth, tenth, first, and seventh
house cusps). And to these he gave the meanings
of suffering (4), action (10), life (1), and
marriage (7). While retaining the twelve-division
counterclockwise concepts of the other systems,
Morin recommended judging a premise on observed
results rather than upon theory alone.

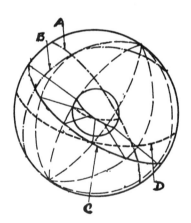

Figure 25. Diagram of celestial sphere with (A)
          celestial equator, (B)meridian, (C)
          ecliptic, and (D)horizon.

Morin was an astrological consultant for
Cardinal Richelieu and predicted this political
leader's death within hours of its occurrence.

HOUSES: WHICH AND WHEN

He also saw the deaths of Gustavius Adolphus, Louis XIII, and Wallenstein. Whether these feats were done by the Rational and Universal Method or according to Regiomontanus is not known.

The only known proponent of the Morinus house system is English astrologer Edward Lyndoe who has formulated a very usable, contemporary system using Morinus tables of houses. Clear instructions for using this scheme are given in Lyndoe's book *Astrology for Everyone*. Some of the major keywords coined for personal delineations are:

                House 1 - Personality
                House 2 - Resources
                House 3 - Intellect
                House 4 - Home Life
                House 5 - Creativity
                House 6 - Nurturing
                House 7 - Relationships
                House 8 - Regeneration
                House 9 - Ethics
                House 10- Vocation
                House 11- Friends
                House 12- Limitations

Other, very able keywords used for mundane judgments in community and world affairs are:

                House 1 - Citizens
                House 2 - GNP
                House 3 - Media/Newspapers
                House 4 - Real Estate
                House 5 - Recreation
                House 6 - Armed Services
                House 7 - Diplomatic Affairs
                House 8 - Banking/Mint
                House 9 - Courts/Laws
                House 10- President
                House 11- Governing Body
                House 12- Institutions

Lyndoe has retained the cyclicity which Morin envisioned as the purpose of horoscopic houses.

As the day dawns, brightens into a productive and vigorous noontime, gradually fades away to dusk, and finally falls with the evening silence and ceasing of activity, so does man go through the cycles of life. In this, Morin saw the mysteries of life unfold through horoscopic symbology. He was adamant about having planets lie above the Ascendant-Descendant axis if they were above the horizon and below if they were below it.

The Rational System of Regiomontanus remained the dominant house division in Europe during this late Classical period. With the coming of the so-called Age of Science, astrology fell into disrepute and many learned texts were lost forever.

British astrologer John Partridge adopted the new Placidian system in the early 1700's, and his concepts were the ones accepted when astrological practice was revived in the late nineteenth century.

Our premise is that the Morinus house system may best be used to show a path of individual involvement into a blending of physical, mental, and spiritual matters. Because the Morinus house circles are really circles of celestial latitude, they are not altered as latitude increases, even at the north or south poles.

Native E is a young man trained in secondary education and certified as a teacher, but he does not choose to continue in this vocation. He constantly rebelled against the administrators in each school where he taught and was generally discontent (Pluto-Mercury in the tenth house in opposition to Moon-Node in the fourth house and both square to Jupiter in the eighth house).

He wants to become involved in metaphysical study, but has not yet made a commitment to any field of study or discipline (Uranus-Midheaven in the ninth house square Saturn-Ascendant in the twelfth house and Uranus in the first house, also inconjunct Moon-Node in the fourth house). He has two children, the first born out of wedlock and has difficulty grasping the reins of fatherhood. The young man's wife respects his need for freedom and responds accordingly. She brings understanding but not money into the relationship (Jupiter in the eighth house opposing Mars in the second house).

Tropical
Morinus

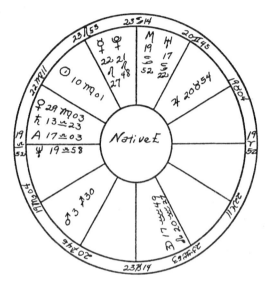

Figure 26. Horoscope of Native E.

Major limitations are need for affection and approval which are unlikely to come, considering his disheveled appearance and constant change of careers (Venus and Saturn in the twelfth house).

At a time when he was desperate for funds, this native moved to Alaska to work on a fishing boat for a season (Sun and Venus in the relocated second house). He appreciated the substantial income, but even more than that he thoroughly enjoyed serving aboard ship with some salty old characters (see Figure 27).

With this move the young man found a deeper pride in self (Jupiter in relocated tenth house), personal power (Pluto in relocated first house), masculine co-workers (Mars in the relocated sixth house), and released some of his inhibitions (Saturn and Neptune moved to the relocated third house).

He returned home with a more mature attitude, greater comprehension that the demands of society are only part of one´s spiritual development, and into a more solvent financial situation. In other house systems, this particular relocation pattern would have been distorted because of domification breakdowns near the poles. The true purposes for moving would not have appeared so clearly in any other system.

Tropical
Morinus

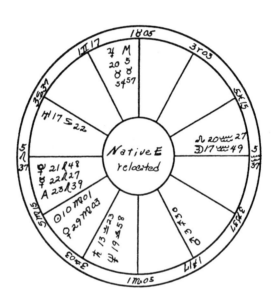

Figure 27. Native E relocated to Alaska.

8

PLACIDUS HOUSE SYSTEM

Placidus de Titis (A.D. 1603-1668) was a professor of mathematics, author of the *Primum Mobile*, and personal astrologer to Archduke Leopold William of Austria. Based on his study of the works of Ptolemy, Placidus believed that he had recovered a system of house division which he thought Ptolemy had espoused, but he only recovered Ptolemy´s method for primary directions. Anyway, Placidus devised a quadrant house system with twelve divisions moving counterclockwise, having the Ascendant on the first house cusp and the Midheaven on the tenth. The system fails in polar regions. Details for constructing these house cusps are found in numerous texts, including *The Elements of House Division*, by Ralph William Holden.

In 1650, Placidus published a set of tables along with explanations for their use. Their later inclusion in the annual *Raphael´s Almanac* guaranteed their popularity, even into the twentieth century.

Although many other house systems consider quadrant and hemisphere emphasis, most contemporary observations are on horoscopes set in the Placidus houses (see Figure 28).

Natives having a majority of planets in the upper or southern hemisphere, from Ascendant (E)

69

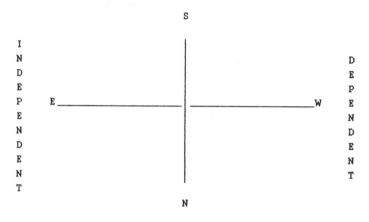

Figure 28. House emphasis by hemispheres.

clockwise to Descendant (W), find that their affairs become public, even if they wish to be private. These people feel that associates gain through them although the reverse is true. One example of this type is given in Figure 29.

Individuals with a majority of planets in the lower or northern hemisphere, from Descendant clockwise to Ascendant, are introverts who collect myriad experiences and internalize them. They rarely express opinions in public. An example is shown in Figure 30.

The people with a majority of planets in the eastern hemisphere, from IC (N) clockwise to Midheaven (S), initiate their own activities and take control of their surroundings. They are said to be creating new karma.

Those natives having a majority of planets in the western hemisphere, from Midheaven clockwise to IC, react and respond to others. They are often products of their times and environment, and are said to be living out past karma.

Houses are further categorized as angular,

70

Tropical
Placidus

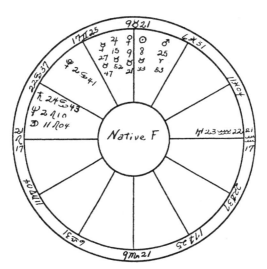

Figure 29. Horoscope of Native F as an example of southern hemisphere house emphasis.

Tropical
Placidus

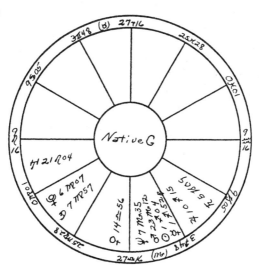

Figure 30. Horoscope of Native G as an example of northern hemisphere house emphasis.

succedent, and cadent. The angles are houses 1, 4, 7, and 10, which are strong and speak of outward activity. Succedent houses (2, 5, 8, and 11) pertain to stable and enduring efforts. The cadent houses (3, 6, 9, and 12) contain planets acting behind the scenes.

Areas of human experience defined by Placidus houses deal with objectives of life, timing of events, and psychological understanding:

House 1 - self-awareness, personal responses, physical movements like walking

House 2 - material resources, innate talents, spending habits

House 3 - method of reasoning, conscious mind, siblings, teaching techniques

House 4 - home setting, mother, family traditions and memories, food preferences, childhood conditioning

House 5 - creative efforts, children, all forms of speculation, preferred entertainment

House 6 - quality of workplace, co-workers, outlets for service, general health

House 7 - legal partners, marriage, methods of relating, public appearance

House 8 - partnership resources, occult matters, taxation, curiosity about unknown

House 9 - overseas travel, higher education, philosophy, personal moral values,

House 10- professional aspirations, relations with the father or any authority figure, social status, honors

House 11- description of friends, general fulfillments, interest in groups

House 12- subconscious, hospitals, personal limitations, deception, secrets, need for solitude or meditation

9

SOLAR EQUILIBRIUM CHARTS

A solar equilibrium chart is used primarily when the birthtime is unknown, but it has other applications as well. A solar chart is not an *hour-scope* but is a *day-scope* in that it deals with movement of the Sun during a 24-hour period.

This type of chart is cast for sunrise on any given day, so only the time of sunrise for a particular location is needed to calculate a rising degree. Since that degree and the Sun placement are identical, they are both placed on the cusp of the first house and then the other houses continue counterclockwise in thirty-degree arcs. There will be no Ascendant or Midheaven.

Solar equilibrium charts are used by writers who prepare predictive astrological columns for popular magazines and daily newspapers. They project probable happenings by looking at every ten degrees of each Sun sign and suggest events based on transiting aspects to the Sun, rising degree, and house placements of the transits.

Arabic Parts can be seen from the obvious relationships between the Sun and other planets shown in solar equilibrium charts. The Part of Fortune is the Moon's position, Part of Commerce relates to Mercury, Part of Love is Venus, Part of Passion is Mars, Part of Increase is Jupiter, Part of Illness is Saturn, Part of Accidents is

Uranus, Part of Deception is Neptune, and Part of
Organization is Pluto.

Solar charts are considered effective because
man lives by absorbing life-giving energy, or
prana, from the Sun. And that energy begins to
flow anew each day at sunrise. Numerous American
Plains Indian tribes had legends about Sunboy
going to sleep and then awakening each morning.
Certain African and Mayan nations celebrated his
rising each morning with major prayers and cere-
monies. Some individuals appear to react more to
this Sun, or ego degree, than they do to the
Ascendant, or family degree.

Each house cusp in a solar equilibrium chart
represents an aspect of the Sun which may be considered as the personality or individuality of
the native in a particular incarnation. Esoteric
relationships between aspects of the personality
are shown in Figure 31. The definition of personality or ego in psychological jargon is quite
different.

```
                      ┌ mental     (houses 3-7-11)
                      │
                      │ emotional  (houses 4-8-12)
SOUL--PERSONALITY     │
                      │ etheric    (houses 2-6-10)
                      │
                      └ physical   (houses 1-5-9)
```

Figure 31. Diagram of the relationships between
           an incarnated soul in a personality
           made up of mental, emotional, etheric,
           and physical bodies, which compare to
           particular solar equilibrium houses.

The actual position of the Moon may vary by
as many as three to nine degrees on either side
of its position in a solar equilibrium chart.
Thus, it is unwise to use this body as a timing
device. It may even change zodiacal signs.

HOUSES: WHICH AND WHEN

Mundane keywords for the various houses of a solar equilibrium chart are as follows:

House 1 - physical appearance and dress
House 2 - income and talents
House 3 - commerce and relatives
House 4 - home and luck
House 5 - fun and frolic
House 6 - health and job
House 7 - partners and legal matters
House 8 - insurance, loans, and wills
House 9 - ethics, training, and in-laws
House 10- government, bosses, and promotions
House 11- windfalls, friends, and affiliations
House 12- hospitals, sorrows, and secrets

The native whose solar equilibrium chart is shown in Figure 32 is a career military officer, gifted tenor whose work is now semi-professional, and clever spokesman, who is also considered to be a handsome figure of a man. He feels fated for success and it is true that "lady luck" smiles on his every move. His rather unusual value system spills over into his marital relationship, where he envisions himself as a proper family man with interesting, but discreet, romantic liaisons in the background. That his friends and wife are aware of these attachments has never occurred to him.

Form and reputation are of utmost importance to this individual and he never steps outside the bounds of what is proper in his outward demeanor. His private life is a different matter. Military promotions and upgraded assignments have come at regular intervals until he now holds a high rank and will retire with honors. His family holds him in respect and complies with his desires. In fact, his wife is happy with their arrangement.

Even if the Moon moved by as many as nine degrees it would still remain in the tenth house of honors and promotions, showing an adoring public smiling upon this native in an open and cheerful manner. Even superiors and associates nurture and protect him.

Tropical
Solar Equilibrium Chart

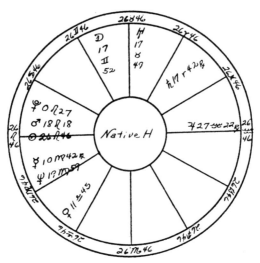

Figure 32. Solar equilibrium chart of Native H.

10

HAMBURG SCHOOL 6-HOUSE SYSTEM

Although Pfaff and Schubert had earlier translated Ptolemy's *Tetrabiblos* into German, the true revival of astrology in Germany was closely associated with growth of the Theosophical Society in the 1880's. Leaders in the TS movement were interested in details of animal magnetism, cabalistic traditions, dream interpretation, and other occult phenomena. A parallel movement was then ongoing in England.

Regardless of the split between Dr. Steiner (General Secretary of the German Section of TS) and the international organization at Adyar, books were in great demand and publication of astrological and occult literature fell on the shoulders of his associate, Hugo Vollrath.

The only German astrology group existing in the early 1900's was the Cosmos Society of German Astrologers, led by Dr. P. Reinhart. The 1920's saw a dramatic increase in astrological study among the total German population. People looked for explanations for their national defeat in World War I and the subsequent runaway inflation. Astrology began to be considered as an independent science rather than a section of Hermetic tradition.

Frau Elsbeth Ebertin was the most active German astrological publicist of her generation and this prolific writer counted kings and heads of state among her clientele. Her son, Reinhold Ebertin, later established the system now called cosmobiology.

At the 1923 Astrologer's Congress in Leipzig, a major discussion was held about theories emitting from the new Hamburg School of Astrology, founded by Alfred Witte (A.D. 1878-1941). Congress attendees were extremely concerned about having astrology accepted as a legitimate science and were willing to go to any length to achieve this goal. Various motions were put forth such as the formation of a central office where data could be collected and analyzed. Headquarters were finally set in Munich with statistical collection offices in Leipzig and Hamburg. Questionnaires were prepared to test the validity of the various Ascendant theories, pre-natal epochs, sensitive points, transneptunian bodies, and astro-meteorology. But, these projects were not completed.

Out of this climate came one of the most innovative astrologers of modern times—Alfred Witte. He discarded many of the current premises and espoused a revolutionary approach to the study of astrology. A former employee of the surveyor's office in Hamburg, Witte served on the Russian front during World War I. During that period he attempted to predict artillery barrages by classical methods and failed. This led Witte to investigate other concepts. After the war he further tested his theories by answering specific questions about timing from utter strangers. His results were amazingly correct. Witte's articles on this new system were published in *Astrologische Rundschau* in the 1920's. In the interim its main advocates and translators have been Ludwig Rudolph in Germany; Richard Svehla in Cleveland, Ohio; and Hans Niggemann in Germany and New York.

Procedures used in the Hamburg School are:

(1) personal points
(2) eight transneptunian bodies
(3) planetary pictures

(4) 360° and 90° dials
(5) special houses relating to cardinal
    points

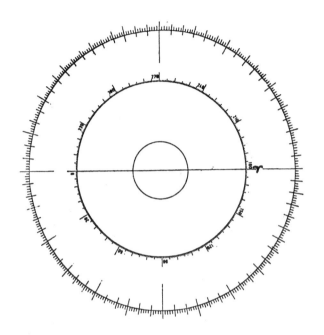

Figure 33. Example of a 360-degree dial.

Since our discussion concerns house systems,
only the rudiments of other aspects need to be
given. Personal points including the Midheaven,
Ascendant, Aries Point, Moon's Node, Sun, and
Moon.

Locations for the first four transneptunian
bodies (Cupido, Hades, Zeus, and Kronos) were
calculated by Witte and ephemerides for the four
others (Apollon, Admetos, Vulcanus, and Poseidon)
were later determined by his student and colleague Friedrich Sieggrüm. Current astronomical
findings suggest that there might be an outer
asteroid belt in the vicinity of where Witte
placed these bodies.

Conventional astrologers categorize aspects between planets as good or bad, but Witte considered the quality of contacts as blendings of the planetary natures. He further defined relationships between planets by algebraic formulae. Planetary pictures and midpoints are stated in mathematical terms with planets being substituted for any given factor. For example,

if a + b = c + d, then a + b - c = d.

Midpoints between bodies are calculated in the same manner,

x + z = 2y or (x +z)/2 = y.

At first only 360-degree dials were used, but now patterns are understood for dials of 22 1/2, 30, 40, 45, 90, and 120 degrees as well. A 360-degree dial is shown in Figure 33. Natal planets are placed along the inner and outer wheels. Next the inner dial is cut out so that it moves freely within the outer circle.

Tropical
Meridian

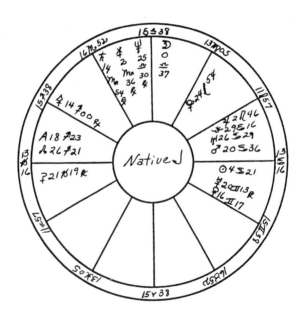

Figure 34. Meridian horoscope for Native J.

Finally, the special house system devised by

Witte involved six personal points as foci. Results are synthesized to present a comprehensive
delineation. The charts are called Meridian, Ascendant, Earth, Nodal or Draconic, Sun, and Moon
horoscopes and are defined by movement of the
inner 360-degree dial. Each 30-degree segment is
marked via Roman numerals. These segments are
moved so that planets react in different houses
in the various charts.
    There are two Meridian horoscopes—calculated
meridian houses and M-Houses. Practitioners vary
about which is preferable. M-Houses are equal
houses beginning with the Midheaven on the tenth
house cusp and moving counterclockwise in 30-
degree intervals. The Ascendant becomes a personal point within the first or twelfth house.
    For meridian, or axial rotation, houses first
calculate the local sidereal time of birth to
locate the Midheaven in a table of houses, then
add two hours to each succeeding sidereal time to
locate intermediate cusps. Again, the Ascendant
need not fall on the first house cusp. An example of Meridian house calculations is shown in
Table IV.

TABLE IV.

Local Sidereal Time	Cusp	House
12:57:37	15 Lib 38	10
14:57:37	16 Sco 52	11
16:57:37	15 Sag 38	12
18:57:37	13 Cap 16	1
20:57:37	11 Aqu 57	2
22:57:37	13 Pis 05	3

Either way, Meridian houses refer to inner
urges and responses, and are read as the manner
in which public successes or failures validate
the native's concept of himself. The major

criterion for judging levels of achievement is
soul purpose (not social values). Witte and his
students were well-versed in the Hermetic tradition and worked with esoteric principles. Meridian house placements for Native J are shown in
Figure 34.

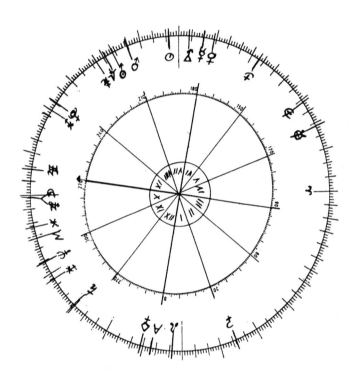

Figure 35. Ascendant horoscope for Native J.

For the Ascendant horoscope, set the inner-
dial house I cusp on the Ascendant and count succeeding houses counterclockwise. These planetary
placements reveal information about his enlarged
family, explain personal relationships, predict
the outcome of one-to-one confrontations, and
describe confidants (see Figure 35).

To locate the Earth houses, place the inner-dial arrow (house X cusp) on zero degrees of Cancer on the outer dial. Remaining houses fall in order counterclockwise. This pattern shows how an individual relates to the world at large. Certain external events pass by with little or no effect while others trigger responses whether or not the native is in the public eye (Figure 36).

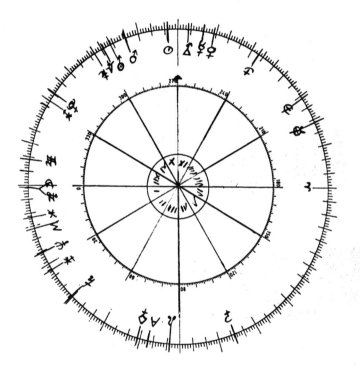

Figure 36. Earth horoscope for Native J.

Nodal or Draconic houses are found by placing the inner-dial house I cusp on the Node. Planets in these houses show how an individual fits into his peer group. They deal with indirect relationships like classmates, co-workers, pen pals, teammates, committee members, fellow travelers, party guests, seminar attendees, joint callers, and connections (see Figure 37).

83

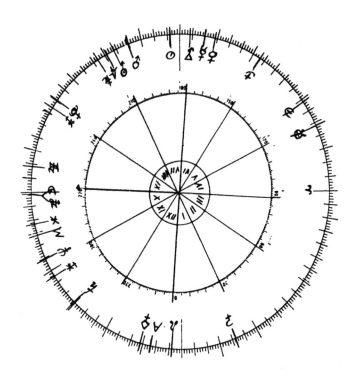

Figure 37. Nodal/Draconic horoscope for Native J.

Sun houses are found by placing the inner-dial arrow directly opposite natal Sun, so the house IV cusp will lie on the Sun. Planets in these houses describe the physical body, outer appearance, assertive activities, health matters, and authority figures (see Figure 38).

For Moon houses, set the inner-dial arrow (cusp of house X) on the natal Moon. Planets here speak of personal likes and dislikes, emotional reactions, attitudes, memories, psychological complexes, nurturing ability and needs, and women in general (see Figure 39).

To summarize, place inner-dial cusps on the outer-dial places as shown in Table V.

TABLE V.

Hamburg Horoscope	Inner Dial		Outer Dial
Meridian	Cusp X	on	Midheaven
Ascendant	Cusp I	on	Ascendant
Earth	Cusp X	on	0° Cancer
North Node	Cusp I	on	North Node
Sun	Cusp IV	on	Sun
Moon	Cusp X	on	Moon

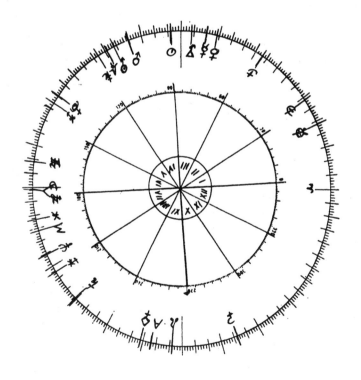

Figure 38. Sun horoscope for Native J.

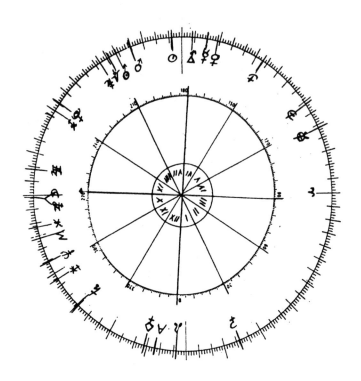

Figure 39. Moon horoscope for Native J.

Planetary interactions are then synthesized from a table of house positions such as the one in Table VI constructed for Native J. Interpretations can be read either for each planet in six houses or a specific question may be answered within the framework of a single house.

A simple interpretation for **Mercury** in this case is as follows. This young man has a logical reasoning process (Mer-6, Nod-6, and Moo-6) and enjoys chatting with friends and associates (Asc-7) as well as exploring philosophical ideas in a quiet and objective manner (Ear-9, Moo-6). He has a pleasant voice (Sun-3) and an extensive vocabulary, in addition to being tri-lingual.

His Juno delineation is interesting. Native

HOUSES: WHICH AND WHEN

J sees marriage as a contract between two friends
who respect each other (Asc-11, Nod-11, and Moo-
11), with each accepting his or her own share of
the attendant responsibilities (Ear-2). His wife
should be an asset to her husband's career and
enhance his professional standing (Mer-10 and
Sun-7). Her dowry and heritage are to be
acceptable according to current standards (Ear-
2).

TABLE VI.

PLANET	HAMBURG HOUSES					
	MER	ASC	EAR	NOD	SUN	MOO
Mercury	6	7	9	6	3	6
Venus	6	6	9	6	3	6
Mars	7	8	10	7	4	7
Ceres	1	2	4	1	10	1
Pallas	8	12	3	12	9	12
Juno	10	11	2	11	7	11
Vesta	7	8	10	8	4	7
Jupiter	7	8	11	8	4	8
Saturn	10	11	2	11	8	11
Uranus	7	8	10	7	4	7
Neptune	10	11	1	10	7	10
Pluto	8	9	11	8	5	8
Cupido	9	10	1	10	6	9
Hades	4	4	8	5	2	5
Zeus	8	9	11	9	5	8
Kronos	5	5	8	5	2	5
Apollon	9	10	12	9	6	9
Admetos	4	4	7	4	1	4
Vulcanus	6	7	9	6	3	6
Poseidon	9	10	1	10	7	10

*How does this individual fit into the world
in general?* From his **Earth** horoscope placements,
it is clear that he is a philosopher who observes

his fellowman (Mercury, Venus, and Vulcanus in house 9), appreciating the various aspects of the human condition (Jupiter, Pluto, and Zeus in house 11). He is aware of current events and travels frequently (Mars, Vesta, and Uranus in house 10) but is apolitical. Native J is intrigued by the inner workings of matters and relationships without being indiscreet (Hades and Kronos in house 8).

Health matters are within the province of the Sun horoscope and this describes his short, wiry body accurately (Admetos in house 1, Pluto and Zeus in house 5, plus Juno and Neptune in house 7). Native J has a compact, healthy, well-proportioned physique and is not interested in sports; he is also the last male of his line (Mars, Vesta, and Jupiter in house 4). Cupido and Apollon in house 6 show the probable longevity he has inherited from both parents.

A look at the frequency of houses posited is also interesting, but there are no set rules for measuring this factor. In this case, house 8 was filled 16 times while houses 3 and 12 were inhabited only three times each. Houses 10, 7, and 9 also held planets in multiples cases.

This technique is interesting and stands up well under close scrutiny for those who have used it. However, it has not been as widely accepted in the astrological community as the predictive aspects of the Hamburg School. Here is a method for analyzing natal horoscopes in multiple dimensions, each highlighting particular characteristics.

11

OCTOSCOPE WATCHES

According to Cyril Fagan, the great Egyptian sage Imhotep (2800 B.C.) advocated the use of a horoscope having eight divisions rather than the twelve-house figure later popularized by Greek philosophers. Regardless of its origin, Fagan and Carl Stahl wrote about an eight-house figure which they called an **octoscope**.

This chart is based on time and deals with mundane matters. It is not a psychological tool, but is an interesting timing device. This figure is comprised of eight spaces or **watches** running clockwise. The center of a watch is its strongest area and is called a **median** or *smedt*. Beginnings and endings of watches are on the cusps. Time is measured from sunrise to sunset:

        Watch 1 - sunrise
        Watch 2 - midmorning
        Watch 3 - noon
        Watch 4 - afternoon
        Watch 5 - dinner
        Watch 6 - evening
        Watch 7 - bedtime
        Watch 8 - dark night

Each watch is named for the events which normally occur while the Sun passes through the hours of the day it represents. Watches then

Emma Belle Donath

stood for activities of simple farmers or peasants:

Watch 1 - alertness, awakening, birth, light,
         physical energy, thanksgiving
Watch 2 - bartering, chores, details of the
         day, planning, visiting, working
Watch 3 - eating, sailing, seeking shade,
         siesta, talking quietly, traveling
Watch 4 - conferring with father, respect to
         ancestors, tending family fields
Watch 5 - children, frolic, fun, joking,
         playing, sharing, talking
Watch 6 - bedding infants, feeding cattle,
         dosing the ill, lighting candles
Watch 7 - bedding the wife, closing the door
         curtain, protecting the home
Watch 8 - darkness, death, loss of vitality,
         quiet, stillness, winds of change

A somewhat modified concept of the watches is needed for today's urban dweller whose day may start at noon and last into the early morning. Each natal octoscope begins with the rising degree for the time of birth. Contemporary keywords may be substituted for those given. Another way of reading an octoscope is to relate these eight segments to the phases of a normal life:

Phase 1 - childhood.......ages 00 to 09
Phase 2 - adolescence.....ages 09 to 18
Phase 3 - apprenticeship..ages 18 to 27
Phase 4 - parenthood......ages 27 to 36
Phase 5 - achievement.....ages 36 to 45
Phase 6 - maturity........ages 45 to 54
Phase 7 - retirement......ages 54 to 63
Phase 8 - withdrawal......ages 63 to 72

The individual whose octoscope is shown in Figure 40 has lived through one round of the 72-year cycle and her planetary placements are good examples of how the nine-year phases correlate with actual events. Each year is represented by about five degrees although that may vary from one person to another.

90

Tropical
Octoscope

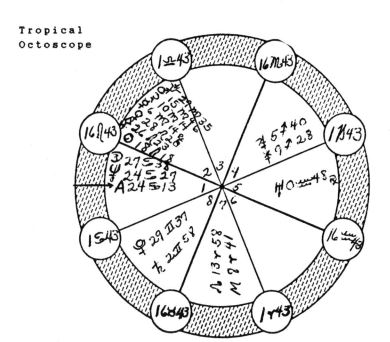

Figure 40. Octoscope for Native K.

Native K was disillusioned early in life by her parent's divorce and her mother subsequent remarriage (Neptune and Moon in watch 1). But, this was nothing compared to the events which influenced her adolescent years.

Between the ages of nine and eighteen, Native K associated with noted statesmen (Sun in watch 2) regularly when she traveled alone (Mercury in watch 2) for periodic visits with her father. Because of a series of operations (Ceres in watch 2) she was tutored at home (Pallas in watch 2). Lengthy bed rest led to chronic nephritis (Venus in watch 2) which continues today. During her early teens she rebelled at the rules laid down by both parents (Mars in watch 2) and became part of an Eastern oriented ashram (Vesta in watch 2) before such things were fashionable in the West.

The next phase of her life was rather placid

for she married a conservative young man of the same faith as her parents and they lived in a peaceful rural community.

During the fourth phase of life, Native K reared four children in a normal family situation. She was involved in school and civic activities and considered to be an ideal wife and mother (Jupiter and Juno in watch 4).

At age forty she had a change-of-life baby in the same year when her first grandson was born. Unusual circumstances surrounding both marriages (Uranus in watch 5) led to these children being reared together more as siblings than as uncle and nephew.

The next phase brought a flowering to this individual (Midheaven and Node in watch 7). As she was engaged in caring for aging parents and participating in community affairs, this woman privately studied alternate forms of healing and types of meditation. Metaphysical interests awakened during the teen years were ready to surface again.

Operations were performed to correct several physical conditions (Saturn and Pluto in watch 8) during her period of low vitality and she has entered her second round with increased vigor and dedication to her metaphysical teaching and counseling.

12

NEW HOUSE SYSTEMS

Several other house systems have been derived
during the past century including the axial rotation house system, birthplace house system, east
point house system, natural graduation house system, topocentric house system, and zenith or hor-
izontal house system as well as the harmonic
charts of John Addey and the locality charts of
Edward Johndro.

Without exception, these astrologers were
looking for better ways to divide the celestial
sphere and more accurate determinations of the
intermediate cusps for use as timing devices.
There has been little sustained effort to determine new or additional keywords for the houses.
The most commonly used definitions are still
those associated with Placidus (see Chapter 8).

Practitioners counseling under the umbrella
of humanistic astrology use, by and large, either
Placidus or equal house systems. A few of them
have accepted birthplace or Koch houses in recent
decades.

So far we have divided the celestial equator,
ecliptic, horizon, meridian, prime vertical,
diurnal arcs of the Ascendant, diurnal arcs of
the Midheaven, and a projected celestial cone of
rotation. Great circles are formed from north
and south or east and west poles of the ecliptic,

equator, horizon, meridian, and prime vertical and then are projected onto the ecliptic to pinpoint degrees of celestial longitude. Yet, the question of how to tie a celestial body to the earth has not been satisfactorily solved.

Part of the dilemma lies in trying to project a three-dimensional figure onto a two-dimensional surface. British astrologer Norman Blundson attempted to solve this problem by developing a three-dimensional horoscope. Texan Kt Boeher devised a graph which visually shows the variance caused by considering north or south declination, especially when planets fall out-of-bounds (see Figure 41). Neither form has become popular among practicing astrologers.

All systems discussed in this book have been theoretically derived according to principles of spherical trigonometry except topocentric, which was determined empirically. In each case, the flow and the cuspal emphasis of that particular system have been noted; and they vary considerably. Controlled studies are certainly in order to evaluate these and other factors. However, it becomes more and more evident that no single house system contains all the answers for either delineation or prediction.

The two remaining systems under discussion are birthplace and topocentric. Dr. Walter Koch of Germany (A.D. 1895-1977) derived a new set of cusps by trisecting the diurnal arc of the Ascendant and projected these points onto the ecliptic using ascension circles. The birthplace division gives a quadrant, time-based, counterclockwise-flowing system which fails at the polar regions.

Dr. Koch´s basis premises were that:

(1)intermediate cusps, was well as the Ascendant, should be calculated for the latitudes of the birthplace;

(2)all house cusps should have the same polar elevation instead of the tenth house having an elevation of zero degrees;

(3)the Midheaven should be related to the latitude of the birthplace;

(4)house cusps should be time related to the

Ascendant and the birth location.

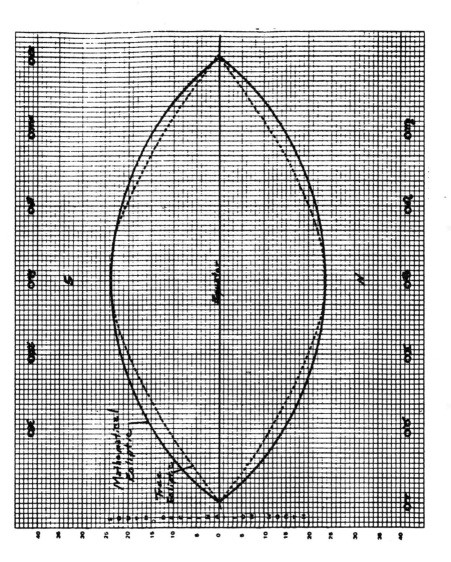

Figure 41. Diagram of longitudinal variations
caused by considering declination.

German astrologer Edith Wangemann worked extensively with the birthplace system and spoke widely about its advantages and accuracy. She promoted the system in the United States and Europe after Dr. Koch published tables of houses in the 1960's. Robert Hand numbers among the prominent American astrologers currently using the birthplace or Koch system of house division.

My delineations in the birthplace (Koch) system for traditional planets, major asteroids, Vulcan, and Transpluto are given in a recent publication on relocation.* There is no need to duplicate that information in this volume.

Over fourteen years of using the Koch cusps, I have found them to be quite accurate for both prediction and natal delineation. Prime causes of failure have been inaccuracy of birthdata. No set of rulerships was considered. This system has been used to deal primarily with immediate issues and concerns. House emphasis appears to begin at the cusp and continue to the next house cusp, especially with sixth- and twelfth-house matters. These houses flow counterclockwise.

Two cases of hospitalization are given as examples of timing of health matters with Koch cusps and transits.

Example 1 - VI/XII cusps = 15 Cancer/Capricorn
transiting Moon = 15 Cancer
transiting Venus = 15 Capricorn
transiting Saturn = Mars$_x$/Neptune$_x$
(bladder surgery)

Example 2 - VI/XII cusps = 12 Scorpio/Taurus
Mercury$_x$ = 12 Taurus
transiting Sun = 12 Taurus
transiting Pluto = 12 Scorpio
(minor finger surgery)

*E.B. Donath, *Relocation* (Tempe: American Federation of Astrologers, 1988).

HOUSES: WHICH AND WHEN

The topocentric method of house division was derived by Vendel Polich and A. P. Nelson Page of Argentina. It is basically a variation of the time-based, quadrant Placidus system. Variations make it applicable at the poles. In brief, the celestial equator is divided into thirty-degree arcs from a cone of rotation (see Figure 42). The resultant ascension circles are then projected onto the ecliptic to obtain degrees of longitude for the house cusps.

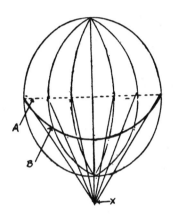

Figure 42. Celestial sphere showing (A)ecliptic, (B)equator, and (X)topocentric cone of rotation.

Nelson Page was born in London but moved to Buenos Aires as a youth when his parents immigrated there. He became interested in the world of business and finance, and pursued those fields in his education and career. Mr. Page was also intrigued with astrology and astronomy, to the point of studying them at length. One of his sons, a nuclear physicist, shares his father's interest in serious astrological research.

Vendel Polich was reared and educated in Hungary where he eventually became a professor of mathematics in Budapest. Like Page, he immigrated to Argentina before World War II and was subsequently employed by a metallurgical firm. Polich began to study astrology in the early 1930's but did not meet his fellow researcher and collaborator until 1942. The two men continued their work until Page's death in 1970. Together they published numerous books and articles in Spanish and English. Their greatest single accomplishment was to derive the topocentric method of domification.

Using an accurately timed birthchart, these researchers clocked a series of events. With the use of primary directions and Naibod arcs of direction, they listed zodiacal degrees which coincided with their results. From that listing of longitudinal positions, Page and Polich extrapolated what the positions of particular house cusps should be (Figure 43). After a series of such tests, they derived a house division technique which would comply with their results.

The accuracy of the topocentric system has been substantiated by such reputable astrologers and researchers as Alexander Marr and Margaret Millard, M.D. In addition to primary directions, they also use ascensional transits. An ascensional transit may be defined as the movement of a planet over a great circle or location line on the celestial sphere. Its placement on the ecliptic must then be calculated.

Duplicates of this test can be carried out with any house system in any zodiac, so long as parameters are established before the study begins. For example, one or two specific keywords should be assigned to each house cusp. Then, those actions would be anticipated or observed for persons with accurately timed birthdata for a given period. If Native X received a letter from her mother as the Moon transited over her third house cusp, that fact would be noted. If, however, nothing occurred when a planetary body or bodies transited over a cusp, that information would also be tabulated. Over a period of time a trend would be obvious. Simple activities are just as relevant in such a test as complex and mighty occurrences. The simpler the study, the clearer will be the results.

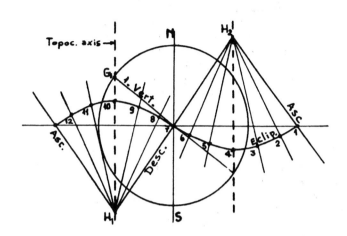

Figure 43. Horoscope houses projected onto the ecliptic from the topocentric cone of ascension, according to Polich.

Keywords for the various divisions of the topocentric houses vary little from conventional concepts:

House 1 - consciousness, head, personality, physical fitness, outward appearance
House 2 - belongings, financial affairs, money, property, salary, theft
House 3 - ballots, communications of all sorts, propaganda, short journeys, siblings
House 4 - dwelling, end of matters, food intake, genetic afflictions, home, mother, oral fixations, security
House 5 - birth, children, core of things, heart, love, passions, speculations, winnings
House 6 - civil service, employees, health, job, nutrition, pollution, starvation
House 7 - agreements, contracts, enemies, marriage, partners, treaties
House 8 - chronic illnesses, colon, death of

99

others, excretion, inheritance
House 9 - diplomacy, foreign travel, philosophy,
religion, sports
House 10- authority, father, head of state,
honor, humiliation, promotion, self-
image, shame, skeleton
House 11- circulation (physical and social), ex-
pectations, friends, support system
House 12- arrest, demobilization, depression,
hospitals, mystery, prisons, scandals,
secret enemies, theft, vulnerable spot

Various researchers utilize different rulerships patterns, but the major proponents of
topocentric houses look at transits, directions,
and progressions to rulers of the houses as well
as to the house cusps themselves. That can muddy
the issue when testing the authenticity of any
astrological factor, whether it be intermediate
house cusps, asteroids, unseen planets, aspect
orbs, or zodiacal systems.

There are other house systems which could be
discussed, but the ones presented here are the
ones currently found on major computer programs
and the ones about which most observations have
been made. Let me reiterate here the premises
made in the introduction to this book about uses
of the various methods of house division:

Sign-House - manner of accepting or rejecting
personal karma, world conditions, and surrounding environment
Equal House - heritage from family members, genetic defects or traits, one-to-one confrontations, and closeness in relationships
Porphyry - clear division between body and soul,
way of compartmentalizing spiritual and mundane matters
Campanus - immediacy of mundane conditions and
how they affect society, and a timing device
Rational - cosmic views broken down into personal
responses, an enhancement of the theory of
"as above, so below"
Morinus - path of individual involvement into

        physical, mental, and spiritual matters
Placidus - goals of life, current psychological
    understanding, answering of horary and
    electional questions, and some timing
M-House - manner in which public successes or
    failures validate self-image
Solar Equilibrium - each house represents a
    facet of the incarnating ego or personality
Hamburg - Meridian = soul purpose
          Ascendant = personal relationships
          Node or Draconic = peer relations
          Aries or Earth = world conditions
          Sun = physical body and health
          Moon = emotional responses
Octoscope - expectation from mundane matters
    of the day, and an aging device
Birthplace - past, present, and future goals,
    expected reactions to events and conditions
Topocentric - mundane events, timing device

    Planetary relationships between each other
will not alter from one house system to a second,
but the house positions may vary greatly from one
division to another. Looking at various horoscopes is like using different buildings for personal needs. One structure is for living and re-
laxing while another is for efficient working
conditions, with yet a third set of walls erected
for worship or pleasure. Determine what you seek
and then build a frame into which those questions
may be answered.
    After a natal, progressed, or directed horo-
scope has been analyzed according to one or more
systems, that data can be integrated as the Hamburg School houses were synthesized according to
Table VI. Each house system or technique is complete unto itself, so that elements of another
system should not be superimposed on it, else
serious errors will result.
    House comparisons for Natives L, M, and N are
given in Tables VII, VIII, and IX, respectively.
In the first case (Native L) all planets and the
Node change houses when comparing Placidus, Koch
(birthplace), Regiomontanus, Campanus, Equal, M-

House, Porphyry, and Meridian placements. Only the asteroid Pallas remains in one house.

TABLE VII. HOUSE COMPARISON FOR NATIVE L.

HOUSE SYSTEM COMPARISON

HOUSE SYSTEM:	PLACIDUS	KOCH	REGIOMONT	CAMPANUS	EQUAL ASC	EQUAL MC	PORPHYRY	MERIDIAN
1	13 ♊ 2	13 ♊ 2	13 ♊ 2	13 ♊ 2	13 ♊ 2	18 ♉ 1	13 ♊ 2	22 ♉ 51
2	4 ♋ 51	7 ♋ 16	8 ♋ 39	13 ♋ 44	13 ♋ 2	18 ♊ 1	4 ♋ 42	21 ♊ 14
3	25 ♋ 6	28 ♋ 11	27 ♋ 51	1 ♌ 56	13 ♌ 2	18 ♋ 1	26 ♋ 21	18 ♋ 53
4	18 ♌ 1	18 ♌ 1	18 ♌ 1	18 ♌ 1	13 ♍ 2	18 ♌ 1	18 ♌ 1	18 ♌ 1
5	18 ♍ 7	29 ♍ 38	17 ♍ 12	9 ♍ 32	13 ♎ 2	18 ♍ 1	26 ♍ 21	19 ♍ 37
6	29 ♎ 9	11 ♏ 24	2 ♏ 5	19 ♎ 55	13 ♏ 2	18 ♎ 1	4 ♏ 42	22 ♎ 7
7	13 ♐ 2	13 ♐ 2	13 ♐ 2	13 ♐ 2	13 ♐ 2	18 ♏ 1	13 ♐ 2	22 ♏ 51
8	4 ♑ 51	7 ♑ 16	8 ♑ 39	13 ♑ 44	13 ♑ 2	18 ♐ 1	4 ♑ 42	21 ♐ 14
9	25 ♑ 6	28 ♑ 11	27 ♑ 51	1 ♒ 56	13 ♒ 2	18 ♑ 1	26 ♑ 21	18 ♑ 53
10	18 ♒ 1	18 ♒ 1	18 ♒ 1	18 ♒ 1	13 ♓ 2	18 ♒ 1	18 ♒ 1	18 ♒ 1
11	18 ♓ 7	29 ♓ 38	17 ♓ 12	9 ♓ 32	13 ♈ 2	18 ♓ 1	26 ♓ 21	19 ♓ 37
12	29 ♈ 9	11 ♉ 24	2 ♉ 5	19 ♈ 55	13 ♉ 2	18 ♈ 1	4 ♉ 42	22 ♈ 7

HOUSE PLACEMENTS:

		PLACIDUS	KOCH	REGIOMONT	CAMPANUS	EQUAL ASC	EQUAL MC	PORPHYRY	MERIDIAN
☉	4 ♉ 22	12	11	12	12	11	12	11	12
☽	25 ♑ 40	9	8	8	8	8	9	8	9
☿	2 ♉ 5	12	11	11	12	11	12	11	12
♀	10 ♊ 53	12	12	12	12	12	1	12	1
♂	9 ♎ 19	5	5	5	5	4	5	5	5
⚳	26 ♋ 30	3	2	2	2	2	3	3	3
⚴	17 ♊ 26	1	1	1	1	1	1	1	1
⚵	18 ♓ 9	11	10	11	11	10	11	10	10
⚶	29 ♒ 2	10	10	10	10	9	10	10	10
♃	20 ♏ 14	6	6	6	6	6	7	6	6
♄	7 ♓ 41	10	10	10	10	9	10	10	10
⚷	7 ♊ 26	12	12	12	12	12	1	12	1
♅	1 ♉ 36	12	11	11	12	11	12	11	12
♆	12 ♍ 0	4	4	4	5	3	4	4	4
♇	23 ♋ 54	2	2	2	2	2	3	2	3
☊	25 ♑ 34	9	8	8	8	8	9	8	9

When the same eight houses are compared for Native M, only Uranus and the asteroid Vesta do not fluctuate between two house positions. Both of these women have worked in a variety of widely divergent fields and have espoused numerous stances. Native L has gone from living as a cloistered nun to working as an appliance sales-person, from writing metaphysical tracts to publicizing environmental movements. In the case of Native M, her career choices varied more than her actual experiences because she had difficulty gaining the various administrative positions which she desired.

In both cases, these women have undergone frequent changes in attitude toward other people, whether partners or co-workers. They have each undertaken to be very supportive and co-operative at times and then have suddenly become quite separative and elusive within a few weeks of making such an open declaration. Dedication and honesty are not lacking; they both are merely acting out of a different framework at various times. Until all aspects of the personality are united as the various planetary positions are synthesized this seemingly ambivalent behavior will continue.

TABLE VIII. HOUSE COMPARISON FOR NATIVE M.

HOUSE SYSTEM COMPARISON

HOUSE SYSTEM:	PLACIDUS	KOCH	REGIOMONT	CAMPANUS	EQUAL ASC	EQUAL MC	PORPHYRY	MERIDIAN
1	26 ♊ 26	26 ♊ 26	26 ♊ 26	26 ♊ 26	26 ♊ 26	2 ♊ 23	26 ♊ 26	6 ♊ 14
2	16 ♋ 44	19 ♋ 52	20 ♋ 6	24 ♋ 57	26 ♋ 26	2 ♋ 23	18 ♋ 25	4 ♋ 0
3	7 ♌ 28	11 ♌ 18	9 ♌ 49	14 ♌ 6	26 ♌ 26	2 ♌ 23	10 ♌ 24	2 ♌ 6
4	2 ♍ 23	2 ♍ 23	2 ♍ 23	2 ♍ 23	26 ♍ 26	2 ♍ 23	2 ♍ 23	2 ♍ 23
5	5 ♎ 25	18 ♎ 2	5 ♎ 50	27 ♍ 29	26 ♎ 26	2 ♎ 23	10 ♎ 24	4 ♎ 45
6	16 ♏ 52	27 ♏ 29	20 ♏ 41	9 ♏ 54	26 ♏ 26	2 ♏ 23	18 ♏ 25	6 ♏ 42
7	26 ♐ 26	26 ♐ 26	26 ♐ 26	26 ♐ 26	26 ♐ 26	2 ♐ 23	26 ♐ 26	6 ♐ 14
8	16 ♑ 44	19 ♑ 52	20 ♑ 6	24 ♑ 57	26 ♑ 26	2 ♑ 23	18 ♑ 25	4 ♑ 0
9	7 ♒ 28	11 ♒ 18	9 ♒ 49	14 ♒ 6	26 ♒ 26	2 ♒ 23	10 ♒ 24	2 ♒ 6
10	2 ♓ 23	2 ♓ 23	2 ♓ 23	2 ♓ 23	26 ♓ 26	2 ♓ 23	2 ♓ 23	2 ♓ 23
11	5 ♈ 25	18 ♈ 2	5 ♈ 50	27 ♓ 29	26 ♈ 26	2 ♈ 23	10 ♈ 24	4 ♈ 45
12	16 ♉ 52	27 ♉ 29	20 ♉ 41	9 ♉ 54	26 ♉ 26	2 ♉ 23	18 ♉ 25	6 ♉ 42

HOUSE PLACEMENTS:

		PLACIDUS	KOCH	REGIOMONT	CAMPANUS	EQUAL ASC	EQUAL MC	PORPHYRY	MERIDIAN
☉	7 ♓ 13	10	10	10	10	9	10	10	10
☽	23 ♏ 39	6	5	6	6	5	6	6	6
☿	12 ♒ 5	9	9	9	8	8	9	9	9
♀	1 ♈ 29	10	10	10	11	10	10	10	10
♂	22 ♑ 41	8	8	8	7	7	8	8	8
⚳	15 ♈ 15	11	10	11	11	10	11	11	11
⚴	11 ♓ 2	10	10	10	10	9	10	10	10
⚵	13 ♑ 10	7	7	7	7	7	8	7	8
⚶	26 ♓ 53	10	10	10	10	10	10	10	10
♃	15 ♋ 28	1	1	1	1	1	2	1	2
♄	5 ♊ 59	12	12	12	12	12	1	12	12
⚷	25 ♌ 23	3	3	3	3	2	3	3	3
♅	0 ♊ 44	12	12	12	12	12	12	12	12
♆	1 ♎ 19	4	4	4	5	4	4	4	4
♇	5 ♌ 26	2	2	2	2	2	3	2	3
☊	24 ♌ 54	3	3	3	3	2	3	3	3

TABLE IX. HOUSE COMPARISON FOR NATIVE N.

HOUSE SYSTEM COMPARISON

HOUSE SYSTEM:	PLACIDUS	KOCH	REGIOMONT	CAMPANUS	EQUAL ASC	EQUAL MC	PORPHYRY	MERIDIAN
1	4 ♏ 25	4 ♏ 25	4 ♏ 25	4 ♏ 25	4 ♏ 25	10 ♏ 46	4 ♏ 25	15 ♏ 42
2	3 ♐ 1	2 ♐ 10	0 ♐ 4	6 ♐ 49	4 ♐ 25	10 ♐ 46	6 ♐ 32	14 ♐ 33
3	5 ♑ 43	2 ♑ 4	2 ♑ 37	10 ♑ 8	4 ♑ 25	10 ♑ 46	8 ♑ 39	12 ♑ 10
4	10 ♒ 46	10 ♒ 46	10 ♒ 46	10 ♒ 46	4 ♒ 25	10 ♒ 46	10 ♒ 46	10 ♒ 46
5	13 ♓ 44	8 ♓ 29	14 ♓ 33	8 ♓ 23	4 ♓ 25	10 ♓ 46	8 ♓ 39	11 ♓ 49
6	11 ♈ 36	6 ♈ 31	10 ♈ 59	5 ♈ 21	4 ♈ 25	10 ♈ 46	6 ♈ 32	14 ♈ 22
7	4 ♉ 25	4 ♉ 25	4 ♉ 25	4 ♉ 25	4 ♉ 25	10 ♉ 46	4 ♉ 25	15 ♉ 42
8	3 ♊ 1	2 ♊ 10	0 ♊ 4	6 ♊ 49	4 ♊ 25	10 ♊ 46	6 ♊ 32	14 ♊ 33
9	5 ♋ 43	2 ♋ 4	2 ♋ 37	10 ♋ 8	4 ♋ 25	10 ♋ 46	8 ♋ 39	12 ♋ 10
10	10 ♌ 46	10 ♌ 46	10 ♌ 46	10 ♌ 46	4 ♌ 25	10 ♌ 46	10 ♌ 46	10 ♌ 46
11	13 ♍ 44	8 ♍ 29	14 ♍ 33	8 ♍ 23	4 ♍ 25	10 ♍ 46	8 ♍ 39	11 ♍ 49
12	11 ♎ 36	6 ♎ 31	10 ♎ 59	5 ♎ 21	4 ♎ 25	10 ♎ 46	6 ♎ 32	14 ♎ 22

HOUSE PLACEMENTS:

		PLACIDUS	KOCH	REGIOMONT	CAMPANUS	EQUAL ASC	EQUAL MC	PORPHYRY	MERIDIAN
☉	0 ♈ 33	5	5	5	5	5	5	5	5
☽	21 ♎ 38	12	12	12	12	12	12	12	12
☿	3 ♓ 47	4	4	4	4	4	4	4	4
♀	29 ♈ 36	6	6	6	6	6	6	6	6
♂	21 ♎ 21	12	12	12	12	12	12	12	12
⚳	19 ♋ 19	9	9	9	9	9	9	9	9
⚴	28 ♉ 17	7	7	7	7	7	7	7	7
⚵	2 ♓ 55	4	4	4	4	4	4	4	4
⚶	13 ♒ 32	4	4	4	4	4	4	4	4
♃	23 ♏ 4	1	1	1	1	1	1	1	1
♄	4 ♓ 14	4	4	4	4	4	4	4	4
⚷	5 ♊ 27	8	8	8	7	8	7	7	7
♅	29 ♈ 41	6	6	6	6	6	6	6	6
♆	12 ♍ 44	10	11	10	11	11	11	11	11
♇	23 ♋ 53	9	9	9	9	9	9	9	9
☊	29 ♑ 4	3	3	3	3	3	3	3	3

On the other hand, only Neptune changes house location when the various systems are compared for Native N. She has been steady in career endeavors as an educator and in relationships, but she veils from the world at large her tremendous interest in, and knowledge about, nontraditional healing methods. Noted physicians privately consult her about such matters, but she has no desire to become known in a public way.

Further analyses of these three individuals may be made by combining the house keywords given in Chapters 2 through 12 with the planetary and aspect definitions presented in Tables X and XI. That same procedure can be followed to give added understanding to any correctly timed horoscope.

TABLE X.

Glyph	Planet	A.U.	Keyword
⚨	Vulcan	0.177	Isolate/Urge to Free
☿	Mercury	0.387	Think/Talk
♀	Venus	0.723	Comfort/Want
⊕	Earth	1.000	Support/Form
♂	Mars	1.524	Work/Energy
⚳	Ceres	2.767	Nurture
⚴	Pallas Athena		Organize/Conserve
⚵	Juno		Structure
⚶	Vesta		Dedicate/Fire
♃	Jupiter	5.203	Grow/Protect
♄	Saturn	9.539	Teach/Delegate
♅	Uranus	19.18	Excite/Innovate
♆	Neptune	30.06	Veil/Dissolve
♇	Pluto	39.41	Alter/Change
⚘	Cupido	42.1	Expand/Adhere
⚵	Hades	50.6	Clean Up/Disintegrate
⚵	Zeus	57.3	Project/Aim
⚶	Kronos	62.4	Elevate/Lead
♃♄	Apollon	68.9	Multiply/Specialize
⚵	Admetos	71.5	Delay/Steady
⚵	Transpluto	77.8	Force/Overpower
⚵	Vulcanus	78.7	Enlighten/Illuminate
✕	Poseidon	82.8	Shock/Transform

HOUSES: WHICH AND WHEN

TABLE XI.

Aspect	Degrees	Waxing or Separating	Degree	Waning or Approaching
Conjunction	0	Unity	360	New Beginnings
Vigintile	18	Launching	342	Culmination
Semi-Oktil	22-1/2	Speed Up	337-1/2	Slow Down
Quindecile	24	Momentum	336	Braking
Semi-Sextile	30	Emergence	330	Integration
Decile	36	Resources	324	Support
Novile	40	Development	320	Nurturing
Semi-Square	45	Upsets	315	Stresses
Septile	51-3/7	Focusing	308-4/7	Commitment
Sextile	60	Opportunity	300	Application
Quintile	72	Insight	288	Talent/Transformation
Square	90	Major Crisis	270	Tests
Biseptile	102-6/7	Zeal	257-1/7	Dedication
Tredecile	108	Cornerstone	252	Unfoldment
Trine	120	Expansion	240	Blending/Absorption
Sesqui-Quadrate	135	Difficulties	225	Agitation
Biquintile	144	Advantage	216	Perception
Quincunx	150	Dilemma	210	Revision
Triseptile	154-2/7	Collective Need Considered	205-5/7	Cooperation
Opposition	180	Encounter	180	Repolarization

There may be no final answers about which great celestial circles best define the human condition until astrologers begin erecting horoscopes in outer space or on other planets. It will probably take the perspective of distance and time to evaluate which, if any, of these house division theories have succeeded in tying celestial matters into mundane or human affairs. In the past, when only rulers and great generals needed to have readings from the stars it was less important to personalize the heavenly dance of planets and fixed stars.

Other divisions of the celestial sphere are possible. The number twelve was assigned to correlate with the zodiacal signs used by Greek and later European astrologers. Early Egyptians and Chinese saw other figures in these clusters of stars. Only the eight-sided octoscope was considered in this volume, but divisions of ten, thirteen, fourteen, sixteen, and twenty-four have been suggested. Anything is possible.

Actually, there have been fourteen official constellations through which the ecliptic passes since a 1928 declaration of the International Astronomical Union. Ophiuchus and Cetus were then added to the traditional listing of Aries, Taurus, Gemini, Cancer, Leo, Virgo, Libra, Scorpio, Sagittarius, Capricornus, Aquarius, and Pisces. Astronomy periodicals often locate a planet as passing through Ophiuchus or Cetus, but astrologers have little noted this change.

Perhaps zodiacal signs or constellations and houses need not be equal in number. A symbolic drawing found among the Qumran scrolls, which were discovered in the Judean desert in the 1940's, shows an inner horoscope of sixteen divisions within an outer frame of twelve. It is said to represent man's golden pathway upward within the structure of ancient Hebrew communal and religious law.

There are opportunities to test previously derived house systems and their components, evaluate the logic of various mathematical formulae used to compute cusps of established house divisions, or to develop new theories based on theory and observation. Doors are open for extensive experimentation and research in the area of house division, for this is an area where questions abound in the astrological community.

APPENDIX

BIRTH DATA FOR EXAMPLES:

Native A - May 24, 1932, at 5:16 am CST
        87W35/37N58
Native B - July 4, 1955, at 1:37 am EST
        82W27/27N57
Native C - December 29, 1944, at 5:45 am CET
        15E31/47N32
Native D - June 4, 1954, at 2:07 am EDT
        80W01/40N26
Native E - September 2, 1952, at 9:36 am EDT
        74W13/40N49
Native F - April 29, 1917, at 11:55 am CET
        16E22/48N13
Native G - November 23, 1959, at 9:58 pm EST
        81W31/41N05
Native H - August 20, 1938, at sunrise
        93W56/44N20
Native J - June 26, 1955, at 7:05 pm CET
        9E04/47N03
Native K - August 11, 1912, at 3:15 am CST
        90W15/38N39
Native L - April 25, 1935, at 7:15 am EST
        75W53/41N15
Native M - February 26, 1943, at 11:50 am EST
        73W48/40N35
Native N - March 21, 1935, at 9:35 pm EST
        84W12/39N45

Emma Belle Donath

BIBLIOGRAPHY

Ashmand, J. M. *Ptolemy's Tetrabiblos*. Chicago:
The Aries Press, 1936.

Bailey, A. A. *Esoteric Astrology*. New York: Lucis
Publishing Company, 1951.

Braha, J. T. *Ancient Hindu Astrology for the
Modern Western Astrologer*. North Miami, FL:
Hermetician Press, 1986.

Bram, J. R., trans. *Ancient Astrology Theory
and Practice. The Mathesis of Firmacus
Maternus*. Park Ridge, NJ: Noyes Press, 1975.

Carter, C. E. O. *The Principles of Astrology*.
Wheaton, IL: The Theosophical Publishing
House, 1963.

Culpeper, N. *Astrological Judgment of Disease*.
Tempe, AZ: American Federation of Astrologers, Inc., 1959.

Dean, G. *Recent Advances in Natal Astrology*.
Southhampton: The Camelot Press, 1977.

deVore, N. *Encyclopedia of Astrology*. New York:
Philosophical Library, 1967.

Donath, E. B. *Asteroids in the Birth Chart (revised)*. Dayton, OH: Geminian Institute, 1979.

_____ *Asteroids in Midpoints*. Tempe, AZ:
American Federation of Astrologers, Inc.,
1982.

Eliade, M.,ed. *Encyclopedia of Religion*. New
York: Macmillian Publishing Company, 1987.

Fagan, C. *Astrological Origins*. St. Paul, MN:
Llewellyn Publications, 1971.

Hall, M. P. *The Story of Astrology*. Los Angeles,
CA: The Philosophical Research Society, 1933.

Hand, R. *Horoscope Symbols*. Rockport, MA: Para
Research, 1981.

Holden, J. H. *Abu' Ali al-Khayyat: The Judgments
of Nativities*. Tempe, AZ: American Federation of   Astrologers,   Inc.,   1988.

_____ "Ancient House Division," *American
Federation of Astrologers Journal of
Research*, Vol I, No 1. Tempe, AZ: American
Federation of Astrologers, Inc., 1982.

_____ "House Division II," *American Federation of Astrologers Journal of Research*, Vol 5, No 1. Tempe, AZ: American Federation of Astrologers, Inc., 1989.

Holden, R. W. *The Elements of House Division*. Romford, Essex: L. N. Fowler and Co., Ltd., 1977.

Hone, M. *The Modern Textbook of Astrology*. London: L. N. Fowler and Co., Ltd., 1951.

Jacobson, R. A. *The Language of Uranian Astrology*. Franksville, WI: Uranian Publications, Inc., 1975.

Jayne, C. A. *Horoscope Interpretation Outlined*. Monroe, NY: Astrological Bureau, 1970.

_____ *Progressions and Directions*. Monroe, NY: Astrological Bureau, 1977.

_____ "The Vexed Question of House Systems," *Astrology Now*, Vol I, No 8. St. Paul, MN: Llewellyn Publications.

Kannan, S. *Fundamentals of Hindu Astrology*. New Dehli: Sagar Publications, 1972.

Koch, W. A., and Schaeck, E. *Birthplace Table of Houses*. New York: ASI, 1975.

Koster, H. *Astrological House Systems*. Concord, MA: Bannister Associates, 1976.

Leo, A. *Casting the Horoscope*. London: L. N. Fowler & Co., 1927.

Lilly, W. *An Introduction to Astrology*. London: G. Bell and Sons, Ltd., 1933.

Lorenz, D. M. *Tools of Astrology: Houses*. Topango, CA: Eomega Grove Press, 1973.

Lyndoe, E. *Astrology for Everyone*. New York: E. P. Dutton and Co., Inc., 1960.

Mark, A. *Astrology for the Aquarian Age*. New York: Simon and Schuster, Inc., 1970.

Marr, A. *Political Astrology*. Buenos Aires: Ediciones SIRIO, 1988.

_____ *Prediction - II*. Tempe, AZ: American Federation of Astrologers, Inc., 1985.

Millard, M. *Casenotes of a Medical Astrologer*. New York: Samuel Weiser, Inc., 1980.

Munkasey, M. P. "An Astrological House Formulary," *The NCGR Journal*. Stamford, CT: National Council for Geocosmic Research,

Winter 1988-1989.

———————————— "The Houses: The Measurement View," *Astrology Now*, Vol I, No 8. St. Paul, MN: Llewellyn Publications.

Neugebauer, O. *Astronomy and History: Selected Essays.* New York: Springer-Verlag, 1983.

Pelletier, R. *Planets in Aspects.* Rockport, MA: Para Research, 1974.

———————————— *Planets in Houses.* Rockport, MA: Para Research, 1978.

Polich, V. *The topocentric System with Tables of Houses and Oblique Ascension for all Latitudes.* Buenos Aires: Editorial Regulus S.R.L.

Raman, B. V. *A Manual of Hindu Astrology.* Bangalore, India: IBH Prakashana, 1983.

Rudolph, L. *Meaning of the Planets in the Houses.* Hamburg: Witte-Verlag, 1962.

Sayce, A. H. *Astronomy and Astrology of the Babylonians.* San Diego: Wizards Bookshelf, 1981.

Schwickert, G. *Rectification of the Birth Time.* Washington, D.C.: American Federation of Astrologers, Inc., 1962.

Shil-Ponde. *Hindu Astrology.* New Delhi: Sagar Publications, 1975.

Stahl, C. W. *Beginner's Manual of Sidereal Astrology, Book II.* Carl W. Stahl, 1973.

———————————— *Thoughts on Sidereal Astrology.* Carl W. Stahl, 1973

Tester, S. J. *A History of Western Astrology.* Woodbridge, Suffolk: The Boydell Press, 1987.

Vaughan, R. B. *Astrology in Modern Language.* New York: G. P. Putman's Sons, 1972.

Williams, LCDR. D. *Simplified Astronomy for Astrologers.* Tempe, AZ: American Federation of Astrologers, Inc., 1969.

———————————————, Moderator. "Panel Discussion on House Divisions," *AFA Bulletin*, Vol 36, No 6. Washington, DC: American Federation of Astrologers, Inc.

This first edition of *Houses: Which and When*
was typeset and designed using *WordPerfect 4.1*
a registered trademark of WordPerfect Corporation
of Oren, Utah,
and then reduced to 90 percent.
Designer: Emma Belle Donath